Devon Hewett

Printed in the United States of America

First Printing, 2018

ISBN-13: 978-1388914448 (Blurb, Incorporated)

ISBN-10: 1388914441

ROMANTIC PROPAGANDA

ROMANTIC PROPAGANDA

DEVON HEWETT

FOLLOW ME
instagram @hewett.vision
art by @claudia_ch_illustrations

contents

Being Human

I am the type of man who is fully engulfed with confliction. Now, what does that even mean? Well, I am so conflicted, that, I have no idea how to express or convey what I mean by saying that "I am conflicted." In a nutshell, I could say, that I exist in conflict because I make bad decisions. In what I feel is the right thing to do, versus, what is the wrong thing to do, versus, *what I want to do*. In this struggle, I have found that my confliction is due to my inability to be concrete in my decision making. I am not concrete because I dwell on the desire on always wanting to do the right thing, but the bad things, remain in focus. Therefore, I find myself in unfavorable circumstances due to factors caused by my own hands. Or, is it because I am just too honest with myself? I have no answer, and that is why I am conflicted.

I think..?

But, what does any of this have to do with this book?

Well, to start, I love being open and honest with myself; and I feel, that this is what makes me human. Sometimes, I like to ask myself, "What does it mean to be human?" "How would you define, 'human?'" I feel, that honesty makes us human because it helps recognize our imperfections. Imperfection, lies within all of humanity, and it is this imperfection, that when recognized, helps us to grow as a species.

Or, so I think it does?

7

Writing, in many ways, has allowed me to express myself when I am not able to do so by any other means. Some artists, express themselves through painting, photography, dancing or by playing music. In my case, I decided to use my desire to express myself through writing because it became easy. I do, suppose that humans are always looking for the easy way out of tough situations. It was always tough for me to express myself. After learning that expressing yourself is healthy, I decided to do so in a way that is fun, exciting and *easy* for me to do. But then the question that then follows was: *"What do I write about?"*

I am engulfed with my emotions, and perhaps this is what makes me human too? I allow my emotions to channel the power within myself towards great and positive things. This is how I got the idea behind ROMANTIC PROPAGANDA. My thoughts, feelings and perspectives, remained locked within my chest, and I had no human to voice them to, or had a human who would stand by, give me their time, focus and listen. These feelings burned inside me, until I was consumed by them. That consumption of emotion, and desire to express in an healthy way, is what gave birth to this very book.

I wanted to combine what it means to be human, with the burning desire within us all to express ourselves. As a human family, we must be careful on how much control over our emotions we have. People, will see you at your worst, and conclude that is who you are. How very wrong such an analysis is! Poetry allows us to unite together because when we read poetry, we begin to understand that in this world, we are not alone in our thoughts and in our feelings. This, in my opinion, helps brings comfort to people. The demand to be loved, valued and appreciated is what I would define as romance. I also feel, that the demand to be loved, is something that everyone around the world desires. In every culture, in every land, in every heart that beats, *everyone* wants to be loved.

I have come to the understanding that romance fails because of the imperfect human flesh. Also, I believe that the human flesh has been indoctrinated to seek superficial expectations in a relationships by a process of propaganda; programming our minds into what is acceptable and what is not. We hold each other to such standards, and when those standards are not met, romance and relationships might become difficult. I wanted to express my thoughts upon this as a message to the world; a warning. My poetry and prose, is a message much different than what I like to call this, "New Age/Modern Poetry." Some "poets," want to write a prose and say something like, "*She found herself amongst the stars*" and consider such a phrase "poetry."

I strongly disagree, and yet many people are influenced by such a simple poetic construction, that they lose sight of what *real* poetry is. When I read something like that, I like to say, "Yeah, that sounds nice, but how does this unite us as a people?" "Where is the substance?" "Where is the value?" "Where is the rhythm?" Or really, "Where is the *effort?*" Unfortunately, in my opinion, I feel, that because such New Age poets receive mass recognition, their prose, *becomes good*, rather than actually, *being good.* I want to take a stand against this idea too. Such New Age poetry is nothing more than a few fancy words mixed up in order to sound nice, but really have no substance. It undermines what real poetry is, and slices the fine line between "quotes" and "poetry." Both men, and women get the two confused, and mix them together. This type of movement is a false objectification of what real art is about. Art is about effort, and such quotes dismiss the idea that effort was involved.

When I read, poetry, I want something that unites us. My poetry is rhythmical, which is an attempt to move the heart and mind similar in a way that music does. This takes much effort, and for this reason, I want the world to appreciate the rhythmical poetry again. This is just my opinion and goal, as I do not wish to cause division between poetry classes or downgrade some else's art or profession.

Although I am a conflicted man, I would never change that about myself. For me being conflicted, allows me to always examine myself, so that I can improve for the better. In the end, I will always know, that I will always make the right choice, even if it is bad for me. That being said, I am confident, that no matter what I endure, I will always come out victorious; because I recognize and accept my imperfections.

ROMANTIC PROPAGANDA, connects we humans together. How so? Each prose, and poem is dedicated to a human nature or emotion I feel we all can relate with. We all have different experiences, and the difference in experiences will help paint a different understanding of this entire book. Together our minds and hearts will flex, and that, I feel, is what moves us all to grow in character.

I truly hope that the words locked within this book inspire much feeling and capture a deep sense in what it means to be human. I hope that this book can help unite us all; an understanding that no matter where we are on this planet, no matter what we endure, we are all the same.

-Hewett

Follow me on instagram @Hewett.Vision

Thank you for your kindness

it is not her existence, but her absence that brings me joy. joy, because i know that this process of pain, brings me much closer to her in my dreams. yes, when i dream of her, only in my dreams, is she here. only in my dreams, our love can flourish. smiling through her in my dreams, is much better than not smiling through her at all. it is the only way i can grab a glimpse of her devilish eyes.

only then, is the reason i choose to sleep. i sleep, not because my soul is tired, but because my soul does thirst for my only beloved whom i cannot live without.

kept writing

no more confusion
i wanted to refuel this ambition
by holding onto the desire
which was to include a new definition
redefine, re-categorize,
what a man will call,

"endurance."

i was so unaware,
too scared,
continuously humiliating myself
during this solitary journey.
for just like my writing
and the congregation of God,
my heart, has been rejected,
unwanted,
and labeled "unfitted."

but i kept writing
kept fighting to prevail,
over the next line of hope.
and yet, to no avail,
it all ended, it all failed,
as quickly as it began,
started off strong like fire,
and quickly ended like smoke

but I kept striving,
kept wiping, the tears of pain
waking up out of bed,
prepared,
to get thrown off this stage
called, "life,"
cold, alone
with bones made of ice,
frustrated, isolated,
finding a new place
to call home?

ready to give in to the pressure,
of this red dragon that floats high in the sky
because this amateur poetry,
and 9 to 5 jobs,
by bike, by hustle and strife
will not allow me to pay rent,
or live a life that a i desire
this depression was a self inflicted oppression,
spotlight on so bright,
friends, family
such concepts
are nowhere to be found
are nowhere in sight
moving along like a snail
crawling upon the lines of failure
so sure,
that being unloved,
by someone,
was my final destiny,

so I prepared to fight back,
and become this war's ultimate victor,
by promising to make my success in the lord
not an option of surrender

by saying, "*grandmother i love you..*"
but this is a final goodbye,
for these hopes of mine
and ambitions have to go,
I can no longer tolerate, this chill,
in the air, sit still,
watching you grow old
as you waste away,
and leave me
spiritually alone
in this
conservative place

13

so here i am,
taking a chance to win,
asking Him, may you deliver
the strength within, to help me conquer
this flesh, within this sin
north hollywood, you're mine
to pursue my dreams
it's time to use these tears of
mine, and my soundless cries,
sort them out,
and morph them into steady wings
so i can finally fly,
for the first time,
to my virgin safety
glide away from the
red dragon floating high
in this sky

may my feet never fail me
may my children,
if I am blessed to have any,
learn how to prevail like me,
let us all hold hands together
for someday, my sweat,
and blood today,
will finally allow my loved ones
to breathe freely

apples, tree

the broken man
the broken woman
are all part of the same nature

two apples of the fallen tree
two seeds fallen from the same branch
so, is it really so
that each one is different?
yes!
for each apple is fallen
then yet picked and harvested
for different reasons
depending on the need
depending on the season

two of the same species
yet, of two very different flavors

letters to men

for what? did you not know, that poetry, is not just equipped for the other species? let's not forget the heart breakers. *rise, my brethren, and understand that you are worthy of infinite love.*

ready, not

i see you
and oh,
i know your pain,
you did love her!
but you, my brother
simply,

"were not ready.."

yes, she **loved** you,
her heart,
bounces,
beats steady,
and yet,
your heart, was
beating off pulse?

you lost her,
her win,
your loss

she found
a new king,
(so she thinks)
a new hero,
(so she thinks)
but do not worry,

you will love again brother,
trust me.

foolishness

men,
don't feel good about yourself
because more than one
woman wants you
feel **joy** because there
exists, *only one*
that is willing
to endure with you
when you are weak,
when you have nothing
when your imperfections erupt
when your pain is heavy
when the chips are down

she's the one,
you want by your side,
not only in the bed sheets,
but upon the grounds of the battlefield

poetry, most

i do find that,
most poetry,
is written for the hearts
of women

but why is that?
when we men, **hurt**
are betrayed, and played,
for fools

yes our species too, *suffer hard*

she says,
"you are not ready"
comparing you to an image of
what she considers a "man,"
from observations in the media,
based on his skin, his height
and his money

do not rush your process of development!

you are beautiful just the way you are
just like she is..

she says, *"i love you.."*
and yet, is emotionally insecure,
will not open up, or appreciate your endeavors.
do not wait, until *she* feels ready,
when she begins knocking
on your door
usually,
when your foundations are set.

19

she says, **"you are my best friend.."**
after you have told her,
just how much you care
and then,
after hours and years of defending her
she falls in "love " with, *another man,*
who could care less about the death
of her mother,
the one you called, "mom,"
the beloved woman, *whom,*
you used to bring flowers for..

you say, *"i have risen out of challenge."*
that makes me a king.
i do not need to meet her expectations
as she is not expected to meet mine..
i have my own dreams
i have my own goals
i am a winner
congratulations
(clap, clap)
(applause)
you have begun your enlightenment,
you have evolved.
and a *true queen,*
will fall in love with your ambition, over your abs
will fall in love with your mind, over your money
will fall in love with your heart,
before you establish your own home

air, same

men,
my brethren
you and i, we
breathe the same air
believe me,
when i confess to you,
my heart, too
has been deceived,
i too have loved,
and lost
yes, i too,
have been cheated, lied to

i lost her but,
she was not worth the fight,

therefore, i have room
to boost about
this very fact:

you will love again

and will find someone
who will respect
and trust your leadership,
without claiming
victim-hood

expectations, don't meet

men, you don't need to meet her expectations, as she is not
expected to meet yours. you don't need to have the career, the
house or the car by age 25. you have been indoctrinated.
if she can be 30+ and still can consider herself a "free spirit,"
trying to "discover" herself and her "journey,"
then so can you.

do not work hark
to provide for any woman who lacks ambition
waiting for you to roll out the red carpet
do you like to play video games?
go ahead.
do you want to collect comic books?
go ahead.

travel the world, have insufficient funds in your bank.
go to the gym. eat hot dogs. watch anime.

who cares? it's your life. not hers. go live it.

a victim, i am not

quit victimizing and self inflicting yourself by saying:
"no one understands me."
believe me, there exists many who possess the ability
to look into your eyes and know what you're all about.

it is not the world who doesn't understand you.
it is *you* who doesn't understand yourself.
and the world could care less about who you are.

however, when *she* comes into your life,
she will want to know who you are, and this
is what will separate her from the world.
this is why you must love and respect her existence.

she is god's finest creation.
respect and honor every *genuine* woman.

kingdom, animal

some men, look at quantity over quality and plead its "instinctual."
because "i'm a man," "i behave this way."
some men use the animal kingdom to justify the behavior
of the male attitude. the male ego.

do not let this be you brothers.
this is propaganda.

if it is you, then understand you have been lied to.
you have been indoctrinated. you have allowed the media's
propaganda and agenda to blind you. what is your cure?
take a lesson found in nature.

is it not the lioness of the pack that does the hunting; not the male? the
lioness, and her pack, risk their life hunting other wild animals twice
their size. with coordination, they attack with ferocity, understanding
that if they fail, their pack and namely their cubs will not eat. the
black widow spider, after mating has the ability to kill her partner
because she is twice his size. his life, depends on her choice,
and if she is having a bad day.

so, if we men want to raise ourselves high because we compare to our
"primal nature," let's do the same for the species in which we all so
desperately chase because of their beauty.

be careful who you chase.
you might find yourself
in a cage with a creature
you can *never tame.*

carpet, red

it is not your duty
to provide to her what
she needs

get a woman on your level!

she wants to grow together?
thats fine.
let's all work together

do not work
sweat
bleed
to provide
for *any woman*

who sits at home, and waits
for you to roll
out the red carpet

kiss
her mind,
not
her lips

allow
her eyes
to become the magic
that gives you
faith

haunted

to all of the men our there
like me, lying in bed,
unheard & unseen
unable to rest, to sleep
whose fleeting dreams,
bleed tears flowing
down from their eyes
listen to me

i am just like you

you are not **alone** in the galaxy
close your eyes
rest your heart inside

i will take this shift.

failure

one day
you will look
into the mirror and
see yourself failing
failure, ultimately is the
greatest expression of the self.
failure, gives the lone wolf courage

get bit by the dogs
and go lead the pack
smile, stay above average
and go howl at that moon

atheism, romantic

"i don't believe in regrets
because don't
believe
that
i'm dumb enough
to make bad decisions.."
(says the male ego)

this is why
you fail to see,
that you,
my brethren,
and your darling,
are never meant to be

that voice inside your head?
thats called
your EGO
yeah,
you need to get rid of that.

beauty, ugly

there is **beauty**,
in the *ugly,*

always remember that,
and you shall
always
rediscover her

pain

her trauma, her pain,
her beauty

respect it, honor it
it is the best thing about her
and she has entrusted you
with it.

her love

respect her love,
never forsake
the rarity of truth:

that out of billions of stars,
suns, and moons,
one of them,
her,

decided to simply love

only you.

evil

there is no evil
in a man.

just weakness,
temptation,
rejection,
hardship,
heartache,

*and **pain**..*

doesn't matter

brothers,
rock hard abs,
fast shiny cars,
sums of money, or
big houses
will always matter
to a woman
but never to one
that's genuine

love, puppy

if she hates you,
then
just buy
her a dog

at least,
he'll never hurt her

dominoes

when she is hurt
upset,
and grows silent

she wants you to *grab her*
hold her
she wants you to *kiss her*
she wants you to,
display your affection

yes, it might appear
to be a game,
but, this is
how she communicates
and if she's worth it,

go on and roll that dice

swords, fighting

it takes courage to
love a troubled woman
and i hope,
you're ready to pick
up your sword,
and fight
for
her

however,
if she lies to you,
forgive her,
withdraw your weapon
and
walk away

can, you

you can do this!
do not be afraid
you are strong

don't be fooled!
your value
is not what *she*
chooses to see,
what
she compares you to
in her books
magazines
and,
movies

do not fall in the trap

the lie,
the conspiracy,
the **propaganda**

that you
have
to
be

like, *"this,"*
or
like, *"that,"*

you are a champion
now get up,
and
conquer

healing

when it comes to healing,
sometimes,
people fall into the trap of believing
that they will never find someone
who will make them feel as special or unique
ever again.

that is a lie.

you will find someone
who will make you feel important again.
you will find someone who will treat you better.

power, man

power and strength
in a man,
lies not in
what he
does,

but lies in
what his
friends and family,
believes
he
can
do

respect,

men,
make sure
she is worthy
of the harvest from
the work of your hands,
no, she is not worthy
simply because
of her
gender

that is propaganda

just as
you are not worthy
of her harvest,
because of your gender

lie, betray

and when she
becomes worthy
of your respect
of your love,

do not hurt her
do not betray her

it takes much
for women
to love a troubled man

support

stop
supporting
movies,
music videos
and magazines
that degrade women

women, lie too

soul, eye

men, the eyes behind a woman
will tell you everything you
need to know

pay attention

men, listen

when a woman denies you because of your height,

understand that the problem,
is not you, but her.
it is just as shallow as another man,
denying her
because of her weight

only difference is,
that you were born this way
she has the ability to do something
about her lack to be in shape

but she doesn't

forever

now, is the time
to **become**,
not the man,

but the husband,
but the father,
but the brother,

you would want
for your daughter

not every woman
deserves such
a man

just like every man
doesn't deserve
such a woman

find her,
love her
give her forever

mind, her

let her mind
be,
your favorite part
about
her
body

love you, she doesn't

if she doesn't block you
three times, hangs up
the phone in your
face, or says
that she
hates
you

she doesn't love you

if you don't miss her laughter
you were
never
in
love

some of the best things
a man can ever give a woman,
is honesty, focus, assurance,
and
laughter

always remember that

we men show affection
for each other
through arguments,
roast sessions
physical activities
drinking beer
and playing video games

this is how we love each other

however,
never allow this type
of love
get in between
you and her.

in other words,
if she wants to spend time with you,
basketball and xbox
with the "boys"
can wait another day

letters to women

you know, the species in which poetry, mainly is
written for; to which, the hearts of men, might
become overlooked.

women, don't believe the hype.
you too have many faults.

love, a woman's

a woman's love is
superior in this case:
that, even
when a man,

is wrong,

she will still love him,
anyway

this truth
is indeed a tragedy
a double edge sword,
wielded, by
the world's most precious
samurai

better, bigger?

sorry women, but big lips and a big butt like kylie jenner
won't promise to get you very far with the *"right man."*
however, it'll promise that you'll get pretty far
with a certain *"type,"* *of man.*

oh? you're into literature and metaphysics.
that's nice.

but, *what else you got?*

plastic

don't strive to be what you see on television. those things are
not important. some of you believe that a bigger "this" or a
bigger "that" will help you attract a man. it will, but it won't
attract you to mr right. mr right is focused on growth and
achievement; and will want a woman who strives for the same
thing. it is evident in how she speaks.

is she constantly talking about the latest celebrity gossip?
or, is she expressing her passion, agendas, thoughts and ideas?

yes, even when you say cosmetic surgery is "just for you" and
not to attract men.. understand that you feel underachieved and
inadequate in your body, because you have been indoctrinated
by the media's propaganda; which sells the idea that having a
bigger "this" and a bigger "that" attracts the opposite sex.

if you are the type to preach to others:
"you are beautiful just the way you are."
now is the time for you to live it.

invest your time in man who will accept you
as you are. *they are out there*

oh, and you don't have to sound smart to be smart. many times,
a normal conversation is just as attractive. shakespeare and
string theory can wait another day..

remains, human

you are not the remains of a failed relationship
you are not broken
your heart is deserving of infinite and true love
not because it has been shattered to pieces
but because those pieces are ready
to make someone else
whole again

tragedy, romantic

do not settle for *anyone* who makes you feel second
place. marriage is not the answer. marriage is not
your destiny. you choose. do not rush a relationship into
marriage because your 25+

do not let the media's propaganda, rush you
into a romantic death. do not settle, when he is not
emotionally mature to only love you. do not give him the
option to "whore around," or get "it out of his system,"

and allow him to come back.

you are a soldier
you deserve better
you survived too many wounds,
to settle for such a tragedy

drama, less

to the women who say:
"i have more guy friends because it's less drama."
don't worry,
i see you
and, i know your kind.
i can see right through you.

you're seeking the validation, your
father/brother/uncle
never gave

redeem yourself

you don't need "more" of anything,
male or female
once you know your worth.

women, stop talking about your ex

ex boyfriends
need not ever be mentioned
on first dates

validation, healing

my darling, you
cannot fool me,
can you?
it is not love
that you are seeking.

the feeling
that *you are needing*
desperately seeking
is not romance,
but
validation and healing
from the species,
that is male
isn't it..?
you do not need his approval
to be beautiful
you shine like the sun
when you seek nothing from a man
not even his romance
go on and *illuminate the planets*

without him

open, book

ladies,
he's an open book
just,
his words are thoughts
of his heart
and
you forgot,
how
to
read

be careful

applause

become the woman
who stands up for him,
alone,
the only one,
applauding for his success
yes, even when he falls
flat
on
his
face..

that, *is love*
and for the rest,
of his
entire life,
you my darling,

will be his to honor,
          love
          and **protect**.

radiance

unfortunately,
you do not shine
because of your gender
my darling

that simply, is not enough
you have been lied to

that is propaganda

listen,
you shine,
because,
inside your chest
beats a heart ready to endure

you shine,
because you have crawled out of darkness,
your beauty,
is your pain.
you're a survivor,
you got this
and guess what?

the right man,
will love you, ***regardless***

beauty, your

it it has become **propaganda**

an instrument used,
to blind your real worth
your access to privilege,
because of the powder
on your face,
blinds you from this scary truth:

that all of the things you obtain,
they have nothing to do with you

nor your heart, your soul, your mind
is not why you are here
you're feeding into the issue

you profess **queenship,**
yet, your makeup covers many lies?
will you ever, walk outside,
embrace, challenge the world
without it?

propaganda,
as if you needed to cover your face?
why cannot your beauty
be appreciated for what lies, **within**?

oh yes, that's it my darling
you are not beautiful
nor are you confident, ***without it,***
that is the media,
propaganda,
manipulating you to buy the paint
you feed right into it.

your beauty is your value
this makes you
unhappy

look deeper

spoons, silver

marry a man,
who knows adversity,
who knows how to overcome challenge
marry a man,
who was fed with silver spoons,
and you'll hopefully
soon discover,
that he was
never fit, to
become your king

leadership, the male

you've never had a father to teach you
what it means to be loved
by another man

do not allow this fact,
to distract you
from trusting *his love*

tree, the abandoned

you abandon him,
*your fri[**end**]ship,*
*your (**real**)ationship*
because you wanted to grow,

but, my darling
oh no,
he too, was a seed!
just, like, you

wanting to become a tree
*waiting for your **water**.*

you outgrew him,
you *"grew up"*
good job.
but remember,

he still has a hold
on your roots
that is why,
your heart no longer beats

queen, you are not

if you are an able bodied
woman,
and yet,
your plan is
to stay home with
your family, and wait
to find mr right to come "*save*" you
that's fine
do what you want

but don't ever profess queen ship
just because you're a woman

he is not king,
because he is male is h?
queens are out building
their own empires

you don't need a man to do it for you

things, stranger

you have what it takes
to forgive the most
cruel, crude of
all men
and you have
and yet,
you feel that
your heart isn't
good enough to
be loved by the right
person.

how strange

implants

breast implants do not matter
to men who seek
to find a queen

what's in your mind?
should be more
than what's in
your chest

growth, her

she deserves to grow
she deserves to spread her wings
she was a soft caterpillar
bursting out
of her
cocoon
her
friends
were jealous of her,
she needed to expand,
and float away to new heights

she will do so, without them
she will do so, without him

broken, women

women,
stop identifying with being **'*broken*.'**
you rise and get out of bed everyday
you apply your makeup, looking your best
you get to work, giving life your best shot
you exercise
you dance
you smile
you are fully operational.

fully engaged.

you are not 'broken'
'*broken*' doesn't work
it doesn't operate
but you do
you're cracked on the inside
and that's ok

you
are
a soldier.

don't attract, opposites

he is everything
opposite
of
what you'd expect
in a man

this
is why he is
perfect

obligation, his

men have an obligation to be leaders.
it is in his
dna to protect
you
it is not a choice, nor is it a systemically
implemented means of oppression or
a "gender role."
a genuine leader must
remain honest, patient, kind,
humble, enduring,
and ready to forgive.

—

most men are not leaders,
not because they are not tough,
big, or strong;
but because they have
not developed or mastered their
most important muscle:

their heart.

propaganda

here's the real truth:

men are cheated on,
and lied to as much as women are
the only
difference, is that men don't
speak about their feelings as
often as women do, so we think it doesn't exist
but, oh darling it does..

it does

it's not in a man's nature to talk about
their feelings
men are indoctrinated
that expressing feelings is a taboo custom

courage, birth

pregnancy and courage,
are the same thing[s]
your motherhood,
is a journey that
a man,
can never take

not just because,
he can not give birth,
but because, he
doesn't have to do so
in a world that
doubts his
strength

it takes, whatever

it takes perseverance
it takes much hope
it takes optimism
it takes ambition
it takes passion
it takes love
it takes joy

for him to conquer,
what he must
every
single
day

his **weaknesses**, are not his **story**
they are the **fuel** that feeds
his **fire**,

know this ladies,
that
if he doesn't struggle with
his character, then
you know
something
is wrong

wounds

your scars,
the
perfect
mascara,
your wounds
the
perfect
foundation,
your tears,
the
perfect
eye liner,
and
the fact
that you still smile?
the
perfect
lingerie

my darling,

you are my favorite cup of tea,

and the pain locked,

inside your eyes,

*my **honey**.*

don't
be afraid
to love his tortured
soul

give him a chance,

as
you would wish
someone else
to give you
the same
courtesy

but,
don't be a fool

don't settle
for someone
who makes
you
doubt
your own
existence

let your scars,
wounds,
and
your bruises
prove
to
you,

that you deserve better

letters to no one

and i do find, that the 'no ones' of
this world, are the souls that cry out,
without a voice

lips, her

when i **obsess** over
the nectar of *her lips,*
i experience
the most
unspeakable of
all pains

for i well know,
that such a pleasure,
belongs to a monster
who
will not hurt her.

too bad for me,
too bad for me

i am not that man

fault, at

ever have the distance, absence or displacement of someone's voice or laughter cause you so much agony within your soul? when that happens, it's best to stop and mediate on why such circumstances bring discomfort. think to yourself:
"why does the sound of "so and so's" voice bring me happiness?"
"why does it bring me pain?"
"why are they here/not here?"
whatever the answer is, may not even be the real truth; and that's shocking. If you're like me, you might over analyze everything you want to digest and consume so you can understand your realm better. this is not always the best approach to life.

sometimes, absence teaches us more about the world we live in, because it gives us time to communicate with ourselves. once we communicate with ourselves, we are able to perceive how we function, make decisions and how we engage will effect how we interact with others.

decoding whether or not factors caused by our own hands may have determined where people we love have gone, will help us understand why we exist in pain. many of us are self inflicting. many of us claim victim-hood. communication with the self, helps us understand the real truth: sometimes we are the ones at fault.
we are not perfect.
we are not free of doing no wrongdoing.
understanding not that "sometimes" we are different and difficult, but that we are "always" different and difficult.
accepting this will help cure the problem.

her silence,
her absence

my cardiac arrest

best fri(end)s

why do they always
come and go?
like a tree thats cut down
and the longevity of its seed
has gone to waste
perhaps maybe they
were never there to begin with?

of course not
of course not

for we are the sun
and their laughter
are the waters that vaporized
the tree's nurture

fallen, the

to the **soul**
who falls flat
on his face

i do not know where you are
your face
your age,
nam**e**,
nor your race

but does it matter?

for this reason,
your humiliation,
your failures and your **pain**,
is the main
reason, why
you and i,
are brothers,

give me your hand,
and i will
lift you up.

superman, the real

he
will
have
it
all,
even when
he
doesn't
have
it
all

it's up to you,
to
find the clark kent

this, remember

someone
out
there
thinks,
that
you're
the
coolest

i know that i do

presumption

(**n**) an idea that is taken to be true,
and often used as the basis for other ideas,
although it is not known for certain.

[aka "what we all, are a slave to."]

what then, is it
that a man or woman can ask for?
it is a lover
it is a friend
it is a family
that never resorts to such nouns

conjecture

(**n**): an opinion or conclusion
formed on the basis of incomplete information.

[aka the "the human genome"]

this dna we call being human
is in effect
an insufficient way of describing
how we choose to perceive this world
around us
for our protection
for our peace
for our security
for our seemingly
greater good

her hair

her lips

her smile

her skin

her aroma

her body

her intelligence

my arrogance

my haughtiness

my foolishness

my thrill

my whiskey

my pride

my **nightmares**

my loss...

feeling, the

you know,

that
feeling you feel,
when you realize
that **your name**
was *mentioned?*

when facts become distorted
when secrets become known
the paranoia from your bones
releases a reality

a reality that you are more alone
than you once thought you were
what is fact from fiction?
it is the burning desire
to solidify what
we already know

and that is,
knowing these humans
next to us
cannot be trusted

the lone wolf

and what made her quit
this chase,
was that she *realized*,
that his dark poetry
and sonnets,
weren't about her at all..

they were about *her*
they were about *Him*

"you, i love"

"i love you.."

"yes, i know,
but darling,
you're too late."
i said.

*"you're **mine**."*

as i chain her
cold hands to the **broken** chair

prescription

therapy, counseling
hospital, asylums
but, they never
prescribed you

you are all i need..

near impossible, damn

i am afraid, of
looking into her
eyes again,
for the
simple
fact,
that
i
well
know, that,
another shot
at rekindling our love,
is damn near impossible

everyone
wants to preach about
"leaving the past behind,"
that is,
until the past
has become something
that is loved much more
than the
present

her *unsureness*
her silence

his **answer**

love story

there is no greater romance
in the universe, other
than the love shared
between you, and
yourself

cups, tea

my darling,
you are my favorite cup of tea,

and the pain,
locked inside your eyes
my honey

taste

i wonder if she tastes
as well as she looks
if her imperfect hair
 really shines like the suns,

or if her soul is brittle like bone?

if so, then my endeavor
is to expose her vulnerability
the secret to my darkest pleasure

my quest,
is to explore and conquer her mind

my love are you mine [period.]

bones

if her bones and ashes
were all that i had left,
i'd dig them up from within
this earth
cradle them
inside my arms,
and sing to them
the sweetest lullaby

act v; scene iv

"almost human"

enter: "the feelings of regret, failed love, failed ambition,
false romance and whiskey.."

we all are so,
"faithful"
when in actuality,
we all are so simply lost,
within the dark desires
of our
own hearts.
like a spark in the night,
what we choose to hide,
about the true,
nature
of our colors,
it is the activity we act upon
that is hidden in the dark.
when our true colors
are opened
and exposed,
our love for each other

and our love
will
become like
smoke

"will become just like smoke"

a fire
that faded away,
into nothing,
like cold embers
from a fallen tree,
our burning and youthful
love for each other,
will fade away
into nothing.
for all that will remain,
is a trace of light
that burns within our hearts,
that when followed,
by a trail of lights,
amongst
the stars,
leads us to absolutely
nowhere.

and still,
we will, all
lie to ourselves,
yes,
will deceitfully plead,
that we,
are all so, *"hopeful"*

amongst all obvious lies

so "righteous"
in our own thoughts,
that we will start,
to retard,
the true feelings
in our own hearts?
because we are all
so afraid of
being alone,
so afraid
of what our sins,
could
expose, about... (us)

and thus,
our love will fade away,
into *nothing*,
fade away,
into *nothing*,
that the trace of light,
that burns within our hearts
will produce a trail
that when followed,
leads us to absolutely
nowhere.

and so we will remain quiet
about the true nature
of our colors,

because we fear,
the pain of loss,
because we fear,
being alone
so in fear of being exposed,
so in fear of our love
fading away

just like smoke

or in fear of what those
we love
would believe about
who we all really are?
would rather gamble with a
chance of life forever,
together,
in order
to live a temporary life
of foolish
acceptance and
adventure, for
the possession of
a smoke that
eventually,
will fade away
just like
vapor

for above all else, and
other things that fail,
there is no greater
form of failure
let it all fade away
as quickly
as it began,
the love that ends
just like smoke

serotonin my sweet love

this paris sky shines more
brilliant than
a september's sapphire stone.
the fine peck of peace
that floats, allows myself
to forget the effects of sin.

enamored by her beauty,
i allow the prayer of tranquility
to begin.

serotonin, *my sweet love,*
come swiftly
and blind my eyes
before me with your aroma
where you belong.
serotonin, *my sweet love,*
can you carry this constant failure
inside my lungs?
serotonin, my sweet love,
can you carry this constant fear
inside my heart.

lovers,
passionate

sad hopes,
broken headphones,
electric windmills,
red skylines,
and the cracking sound
of the earthen soil
beneath my feet,
are the echoes
the melodies,
the memories,
of our hidden sins, hidden lusts,
our empty
imaginary bed,
and our sweat soaked sheets

just like
a glass, of red wine
splashed upon
the sheets of
your first first wonder,
ignoring
this chilling fulfillment,
focusing only on
the thrill *ahead,*
and how we mask this pleasure

so whisper my name, when
you walk through the door,
so the sound of our drunken
jukebox and broken record players
can finally begin to roar

if you're not in 'love'
stay where you are,
if you're not in 'love'
stay where you are,
if you're not in 'love'
please,
stay where you are

for i am forewarning you
to avoid the path of sin and regret
the smell of burning defeat,
locked within your heart,
the sounds of rusted love letters
and the feverish glow, *of weathering roses*

by our lips, tongues
and by our smiles,
we, were such,
terrible liars,
denying what we felt inside,
but by the lust locked within our eyes
we were still very much, "in love"
such, passionate lovers

we were such,
terrible liars
we, were such,
passionate lovers,

so whisper my name,
when you walk
through the door,
where our drunken jukebox bodies
and broken record player voices
can finally begin to roar

if you're not in 'love'
stay where you are,
if you're not in 'love'
stay where you are,
if you're not in 'love'
please, stay where you are

before you are awoke,
cold and alone,
on your cluttered bed
with burning tears,
flowing forth from your eyes,

your teeming youthful heart,
habitual, harmful,
and
hurtful words
will become effortless as we fall
all together

because we,
were such,
terrible liars.
we, were such,
passionate lovers
we, were such,
terrible liars.
we, were such,
passionate lovers

so whisper my name,
when you walk
through the door
so the sound
of our drunken
jukebox
and
broken record players
can finally begin to roar

heed this warning:

if you're not in **'love'**
stay where you are,
if you're not in **'love'**
stay where you are,
if you're not in **'love'**
please, stay where you are

the lies behind the smiles

while paris city sleeps,
i alone find myself,
cloaked,
lost
within the dawn
of this new twilight,
over this valley
the sound of church bells,
and some insomniac poetry.

i could gladly fly away
into the most romantic
of all cities
and yet,
my traumatic blackest secrets,
will still imprison me?
yet i am left to wonder,
why is it,
so much trouble,
for two friends
who really love each other,
to say
what they truly feel?

whenever
things are at their best?
whatever
lies behind the smiles they make,
just so, the other soul,
can safely rest?
whenever
things are at their best,
why do we all wait
after the failed tests
and for all the good things
to simply fall apart?

welcome
to the fallen grace, and
embrace the bitter aftertaste,
of cheap wine,
and bad decisions
when the youthful heart
trembles, in its
midnight to
morning prayers

i could shield my eyes,
from these inner most
seductions,
and yet,
somehow you,
still find my goodness
everywhere?

once again,
this city makes me wonder,
why is it so much trouble,
for two friends,
who really love each other,
to say,
what they truly feel?

117

whenever,
things are at their best?
whatever lies behind the smiles
we make,
just so, the other soul,
and its heart,
doesn't break
and can safely rest?

and yet,
it is my mistake
to say:

"i am not the heart's safest bet,
or the greatest card,
in your hand to play,
nor have i've never been
too good at playing
by the rules.."

whenever,
things are at their best,
why do we all wait
after the failed tests,
and for all the good things
to simply fall apart?

before we announce what it is,
that is truly inside our ambitious love

love, silent

in your absence,
your silence likes to
speak aloud,
about
how you want to say,
"this is the end,"
but when i look into
your eyes,
i know,
this is not the end

our lips took a picture of heaven
when we broke down,
across this silent night,
below the crimson skyline
my mind will not forget,
the colors of our skies,
that forced our
silent eyes to speak out loud

we have missed the point
of living,
so caught up
in this moment,
we threw out all
our convictions,
and traded
them for a lack of confidence
within, this dark space
this chilling substance
called "silence"

if this is "life,"
i hope to fill it inside
with the tears
of our eyes and
draw a new line,
called, "hope"

and so it goes,
no we won't let go,
if you were alive,
my reach
toward the stars of the skies,
would be my final attempts
of my life,
to grab hold of your precious,
beautiful eyes
that reflect the moonlight
above these hills
that cry,
for us to embrace
and dance in their luxury

just open up your mind,
and pay attention
to the colors of the skies,
there you
will find the rain
pouring from the darkest
corners of my mind
the tears of my eyes, that
will forever cry,
cry yes, for only,
you

we have missed the point
of living,
so caught up
in this moment,
we threw out all
our convictions,
and traded
them for a lack of confidence
within, this dark space
this chilling substance
called "silence"

this time, we
have found a frame
of mind,
while you sleep underground,
i will try to seize
the opportunity
to blind my mind
from seeing the stars
in the sky
that resembles your
eyes that shine
more brilliant
that these northern lights

if we paid more attention,
to each other's final heartbeats,
then possibly,
miraculously,
we finally,
could gladly
have broken
free from
this silence,
this blindness
this substance,
called, "life,"
and been able to
finally greet
the sunrise

your breath is gone forever
but it is your soul
that haunts
then pleases me
in my dreams
for i have you still
and your silent eyes
in the night sky
are better than nothing at all

mountain love

i suppose this is how the story ends
when two lovers
originate as friends
all that power
all that time
vaporized into dust
a forgotten ambition

what then,
can two best friends
who really love each other
ask for?

it is that no matter what happens
no matter what we endure,
our love for each other
will forever prevail

that no matter who they love
they will always love you
a level of love solidified like
the way a rock solidifies a mountain

the smell of her innocence,
becomes a familiar fragrance
that fills the air
inside this room,
thoughts of
the unthinkable
and
thoughts of the
impossible,
combined with the sound
of teardrops landing softly,
upon the floor

and so it
ends
like it began

there, her casket
lined with the pills
of her suicide,
and the bitter aftertaste
of my silent regret
to wash them all down

and so it ends like it begins!
by the spark of a flame
alongside this
hidden sin
where not even
holy scripture,
can cure what has been
cracked and faded within

there her ashes will remain, for
all bodies do return to this dust
and in front of this
new monument
of a new hope
i will still much rather
trade places with her,
and drown inside the anguish
of her expired,
ambitious heart

now a new dawn
has broke this morning,
and in my dreams
i hear your soft tears
raining inside this room

as pure as spring mountain water
that could reflect
the beautiful images
of you..

your hope is like a newborn child
so young and oh,
so precious,
so beautiful,
but just like a newborn
you were left lost,
in this world alone,
forsaken,
thrown in the bitter cold

and if i could have my way

we would wake up on the day we met,
to a place where
i can stare inside
your virgin heart for hours
and try to make you hear
the sweetest thoughts

but not tonight,

because you've gone to rest,
forever, underground
and yet, i would still
much rather have your
bones,
wrapped inside my arms

where we could revel in our last embrace

there, i'd steal
the breath right from your lips
and kiss you softly
as we both perish
together

i will rest my lifeless,
hand
upon your heart

forever,
and there,
perhaps
i can find true love
once again,
and
maybe
yes, maybe

i will greet the sunrise after all

new terror

my life was a vapor,
until i held your hand
the voices inside my head
finally grew silent
and i was able to sleep
in what seems like ages
i am able to see the sun

i now stand defenseless
deep in your eyes

the early departed,

a

poem for

all of these useless
feelings *of us,*
the illusions of our
possible joy,
and the dreams of
our impossible future,
are still
haunting to *my heart*

dim the firelight,
the burning fire
of our passion,
let's extinguish this
bonfire of our love,

make amendments with
our past affection,
for our unity together,
are no longer in harmony
like the stars
in the night sky
of heaven
above,
find new ways to be happy
for this path of life forever
is no longer for you and i

but i still know that you
exist in my lungs
for when i breathe
my heart continues
to beat *for you,*
and my tears continue,
to bleed
through my eyes

in my nightmares,
you hold my arms
as i grasp your tender hand,
you kiss my lips,
and then,
i wake up *exhilarated*,
astonished, inspired,
suicidal,
then in constant pain?
realizing that you are
not by my side, no longer here,
again,
there is no greater agony,
no greater pain,
how can love vanish
as quickly as it began?
from the midnight sun
to the morning moon,
one man, one woman
will possess the will
to make their love replenish
again..
i want that to be us,
but, my darling,
it is not the truth

i desire that type of
love, between us,
to become
the rope that binds
our hearts together
forever for eternity

oh, how i wish!
that this,
forbidden intimacy
can exist without the barriers
of our doubts, without the
confinements of
our fears

for you, my
only beloved,
are
the one who,
makes me afraid to sleep,
because when,
i dream,
i dream of only you

and
if i could
have my way,
i would choose
insomnia forever
if it meant,
that i,
could no longer
dream of a world
with you
in it

your love is like a garden
your arms around me
have grown tighter

my love,
may you never forget my name
when the morning dawn wakes us
the strength in my chest has withered,
but that is ok

because your whispers through the night
silence the dragons

night,
welcome
the

if your life were a dream,
so infinite,
always beautiful
and glad,
its brilliance and joy would
surround you,
with pleasurable hearts,
and outstretched arms
a reality unseen,
only visible
in dreams
never
sad,

for its reality will be seen,
upon your limitless desires
of peace and refreshment,
for such an entrancement,
such an embracement,
cannot be,
placed on hold

so welcome the night,

yes,
welcome the night
for it is just the start
of your joyful journey,
where your heart finally
embraces love,
and
tranquility's nectar
while you dream, and
your aspirations become real
to a place where true love
is pure as rain,
and it is
experienced and can,
finally feel real

when everyone goes to sleep,
insomnia rises, and
just like the fleeting sun,
some stay awake
and embrace,
the crisp cold air
locked within their lungs
so they can finally
breathe, dream,
and enter the infinite reality,
of their happiness
a reality unseen

is life just a passage?

where we are all, immobilized,
by the light of the moon, staying awake?
what if the real journey
was in our dreams?
and the true life,
was spoken only
under the breath of the stars,
and this darkness,
locked
within our hearts,
became the very shadows,
turned into joy,
and flourished
like a sunflower's
delightful
winter bloom?

yes, welcome the night
yes, welcome the night
enter the infinite dream
yes, let us escape to a place,
where sorrows and sadness,
have no chance to grow

yes,
enter the infinite dream
where true lovers,
where true friends,
exist beyond the graves
of their broken hearts,
and sorrows
have,
no room,
to grow
under
this
sun

welcome the night,

for its arrival,
is the beginning of joy
and of a happiness
unimaginable
for those
whose only survival
is to sleep forever,
and enjoy
peace
at
last
under
the silent moon,
that shines above the snow

the last, last phone call,
        far from,

here's a long and evasive story,
of a young man's failed hopes
and glories,
combined with lies
from the outward cries
off lips, off the tips
off of broken wine glasses,
and a few scratched out 45's
a loss of godly acceptance,
combined with a list of intoxicated
confessions,
his heartless soul shall be drowned
in this shameless rapture tonight

no, i will not lie
no, i will not lie
no,
i will never lie to you..
so believe me when i say,
that, "i'm trying hard today,"
but, i realize that i may,
never be right for you

no, i am not right
for you,
maybe you and i will see
that it was never meant to be
but it is me

the sins of the faithful,
and the luxuries of regret,
in the end,
it's the faithless,
who will know love's tragedies

no act of purification,
even with all it's best intentions,
no amount of reconciliation,
or processes of redemption,
by means of excommunication,
by means of disfellowshipping,
will ever cure me, of
these feelings of this
godly inadequacy

yes, it is because of i,
that the reason why,
why we will never try
again, is behind all the lies of
your painful outcries

we are no longer one
before our journey has even begun
and even down to this day,
i cannot believe,
that you say,
by your silence,
absence,
and display,
towards my isolation,
and my pain,
that to my dismay,
you believe,
we better off this way?

but i realize
that i am not right
no, not,
right for you
no,
i am not right,
not right
for you

so please tell me, what
you see, when
you stand still,
and look
at me?
or is it enough
to know,
that i desperately
need to sleep,
forever, with you?

so sorry when i say
that "i may still love you"
even through this pain

but in the end can you forgive me?

when i am found alone on this journey?
or on the outskirts of my faith?
doubled up on sins regrets,
alone,
crying on my knees

awaiting, for some god
named, 'Jah,"
to come, and save
this lifeless soul in need?

and in the end
my spirit will write these words,
as my heart no longer beats,
thus my heart of stone
shall no longer be pleased
to beat for you,
endlessly

just please, believe
me when i say,
"that i am trying my hardest today."

in this found year of our lord
i will live, but die inside
knowing now,
he and i
are not your only sons

the faintest sounds of winter

euphoria

the sea has become,
more profoundly red
than a drunkard's favorite,
glass of foreign wine,
these open skies
combined,
with the flare of,
the bleeding sun symbolize,
my fleeting passion
tonight,

so pray for my
sweet euphoria
for her light
is constantly blinding,
to me,
for she feels,
more comforting than-
a grandmother's warm embrace,
more comforting,
more soothing,
than these malibu waves
beneath my feet

in my defeat,
in my shame,
only luxury,
without her presence
and affection,
is that my poor
exasperated heart,
will feel just as lonely as this sea
so let us gaze out upon
these crashing waves
where together our hope
and our love
can never fade or expire away

my sweet,
terrible, angel
please embrace my soul
with your virgin love,

for there is this
honesty,
that has sunk my lungs
and it is itching,
dying,
desperately,
trying to get out
but without your love
and affection,
i will feel
just as helpless
as an orphaned child

so can you carry this
loneliness,
inside
my lungs?
can you carry this
loneliness inside
my heart?

come fast my darling

euphoria..
euphoria..
euphoria..

can you deliver my heart
from this sadness?
euphoria,
hurry to save
my soul,
from these agonizing
thoughts

my sweet angel euphoria
my lonely heart
will wait,

for you

my soul will,
anticipate,
and hopefully gravitate
towards
your arrival
my dear sweet euphoria
continue to
make
my crooked walks,
my paths straight,
my dear sweet euphoria
hurry fast
my only beloved
oh,
please do not delay

requiem on the clouds

and although
your arms and legs
are under,
love will be the cure,
the thunder
that wakes
you up from
this monotony,
called "life"
it is the answer
that silences
this illness called "doubt"
called, "uncertainty",
that of believing
that you are
not
worthy

of all that is to come
until we stumble backwards
someday we must go
and then my love
will be there still

act v, scene iii

"redemption"

enter: human nature, failure, imperfection,
relapse, feelings of rejection.. and sin.

again, begin again and

my heart has traveled, to each
of the ends of
this earth, with,
nowhere else to go,
my heart looked back
in amazement,

until i finally realized
how far it was
that my heart has
actually strayed away,
when in all actuality,
i was still standing
in the same place
that i started until,
i fell down, and
i cried out
to Him

but there was this silence,

a profound,
most definite,
silence and
it was more brilliant
than anything

then
there was this bird,
with feathers,
bright and red,
as the bleeding sun,
at least,
that is what my eyes did see
but,
what my heart saw
was an angel,
on the whitest november's morning

and i heard her sing the sweetest cry,
as if she wanted to reach down,
and tell me:
"it will all be alright"
and then i knew,
my prayer was answered

for i then knew, that
"it will all be alright"

i walked out,
and stared into the midnight sun
i was blinded, yet,
enamored by her beauty
till I fell down, again
and i cried out,
to Him,
and yet, again,
there was this silence

a profound,
most definite silence
and again,

it was more brilliant than anything

once again then,
there was this bird,
with feathers, bright
and red,
as the bleeding sun,
at least,
that is what my eyes did see,
but,
what my heart saw was an angel,

on the whitest november's morning

and
i heard her sing,
the sweetest cry,
as if she wanted to reach down,
and tell me:
"it will all be alright"
and then I knew,
that my prayer was heard,
answered,
for I then knew,
"it will all be alright"

like foreign train tracks
that lead you to nowhere,
the sound of the oncoming train
will still warn you from making
the same mistakes
that is,
if you listen
so, never
take chances,
never embark on,
more than one,
journey alone

for, at least,
each path will
lead you to the rise
of the new crimson sun,
in the morning

you may close your eyes,
walk blindly down
the tracks
of life, and
still find
the sound of warning
coming from the train.

possible, impossible

afraid to live and look
into the mirror
 it will hurt
but will take much courage
but i will be glad
to finally meet me

for whom i really am,
for whom i am to others

if what matters to the world
is something
that matters to me
if the brain is in control,
then reality is only what i can see

and not what i choose to be

i need to stop becoming afraid
of the possible
i need to stop becoming comfortable
with the impossible

stop believing in the comfortable
and start believing
in the unfavorable

handshakes, secret

copper and cobble,
marble stones,
of this notre dame cathedral
built by the hands of
the hidden unknown
twenty years before
this embryo was made

we will make, "good men better."
we will make, "good men better."

but, oh heavenly father
how do you make,
"a good man..better?"

we will make, "good men better."
we will make, "good men better."
but, oh heavenly father
how do you make,
"a good man..better?"

flashback, 33 degrees
the coldest night of their unexpected lies
and of their religious hypocrisy
from this bitter cup
of this Christ
which they forced us all to drink

there i am, awake, its 3:33 am
and it's getting late,
only six years old
and I can tell that
something
in the air
just isn't right..

147

"we will make, good men better"

but, oh heavenly father,
how can you make,
"a good man,"
"better?"

you sign this 'contract'
with his blood,
write his firstborn son's
name above
this dotted line,
so that he will forever hear
their shadows
calling for him in the night

"get up,"

"get out" my son
the fire is
breaking out,
hurry, out the window!
look away, before
you witness, her devastation,
look away, before
you witness, her shame

before your body turns into
a pillar of salt,
or worse,
before your body burns to ashes
a place where their,
bodies are
scattered, by

the four winds of heaven

fifteen years later
i received the book
took upon this
new education
with your disapproval
awakened the new visions
a new perspective
of what it means
to hope, and
what it means
to love again

we will make, "good men better."
we will make, "good men better."
but, oh heavenly father
how do you make,
"a good man..better?"
no answer

and yet-
does it ever
even faze you,
that your grandfather's
involvement with
an underground cult-
nearly killed
your firstborn son?

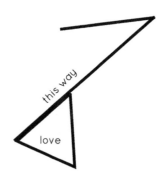

149

escape

a great medicine
is not always
something
that a great doctor
can prescribe
sometimes, the best cure
is to venture out into the unknown
alone
and leave everything behind

no family
no friends

just leave it all and go

it is the closest thing
one can be-
into becoming like a bird
so with your wings
fly
and escape
meet new faces
see new places
and change your perspective

escape routes

and
he will keep
on *drinking*,
because
he
loves the escape..

and
he will keep
on *laughing*,
because
he
loves the escape...

and
she will keep
on *dancing*,
because
she
loves the escape...

and
she will keep
making male friends,
because
she
loves the escape...

they want each other
to
stop
because
they hate
each other's escape..

enter "the sickness..."

what is that links
all of mankind
together?
what is it that we all share?

it is this sickness,
this curse,
this pain we
call,

"hurt"

and the cure?
"the demand to be loved"
a false
antidote

cure, the

i
need
a
cure
for this
form of *cancer*
i've been cursed with
constant feelings of failure.
my vision's weak,
i can't believe, my heart
has been *deceived*,
from a disbelief;
simply, searching for an
answer

so once again
i'm left with
only me,
and my pain refuses
to *leave,*
i cannot believe,
i didn't see,
this moment
come so,
fast...

she has been
swimming through
my veins,
and my biggest complaint
is that my confidence
endurance
and self preservation
will not allow myself to even
take a sip, a drink
in order *to escape,*
and kill this pain;
which are the very thoughts of her

what about this "cure?"

which, might as well,
become the very elimination of
the very thoughts of her?

how can i escape

this trap,
this illusion?

the decision to flee
from the seclusionary
exlusionary, mental image,
of her hand grasping mine?
oh, how
i can never forget!
yet, i so desire to
because,
simply the thought
of you creates a smile
inside my chest,
making me
feel, crazy
so desperate?

do i need another monster?
another criminal
to rob my heart
of what it
beats for?
do i need that
someone
to replace this pain?
so i can forget
the heartache,
of missing a beloved
best friend

the one,
whose very name
causes me to stand
so still,
and cause
my heart to ache?
then break?

what about this "*cure*?"

like a sickness
that evaporates,
the heart's burning desires,
and wishes,

this sickness,
blemishes,
the reason for my heart
to remain motivated,
focused,
and desirous for
something far greater

this sickness,
diminishes,
my soul from
flourishing, remaining desirous
leaving it malnourished,
delirious, curious,
and thus remaining at a constant
frustration

but the fight is never over
for i never, or
would i ever,
choose to walk away
and accept her pain
as a lone soldier against the wind

what about this "*cure*?"

it is the hope for
a better tomorrow
the *desire*
to become stronger
than yesterday's
groaning sorrow,
with or without
her,
the angel of my nightmares,
the biggest success,
over failure
is this:

never remaining
afraid of the
past,
never surrendering
to self inflicting
cowering
of your own
illusionary,
terror

stand tall,
never be afraid
to fail,
to fall..
for the cure
over this sickness
is the desire
to embrace
the
falling rain
and become
stronger forever

awake, wide

times change people
and friends,
change more,
the more you know
yourself,
the more chance
you'll have
to finally win this war

too many problems
too many people
who have the solutions
but both are
nothing but
opposite ends of
the equation,
a nuisance

so we're going
to shut this door for more,
we're going to
change our minds
and look inside
ourselves
and find the will to,
be strong
and carry on

in this dying world,
we all are
so much more,
than fashion
than luxury,
the millions
of things we can't afford,
you must find a way,
to break down this door,
then, you'll
find yourself
in a brighter world

wide awake
we all dream of a place,
where, fri(end)s and
fam(i)ly,
are never ripped apart
or are forced
to go their separate ways

don't push away
another's problems you don't have,
can't imagine,
tolerate,
embrace,
or appreciate,
what it may feel like
to endure
the lifelong torment
of solitude,
loneliness
and
misunderstood pain.

we must find a way
to break down this door,
then,
you will find yourself,
winning against this war,
and find
yourself in a brighter world

look inside yourself,
and find the will
to, place your faith
against time,
fight, dry
your tears away
from your hidden fears,
and exposed cries

by saying
they are not the only ones
who possess the pain,
you eliminate,
any trace
of hope and trust
in you;

which
is why they
may choose, to
label you
as, "the same,"
so go away, and
save your opinion,
until you find
a new
way to break down
this door.

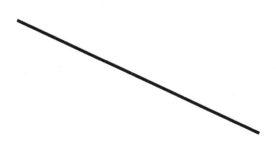

my sweet love, serotonin

this paris
moonlight sky,
shines
more brilliant than
a september's
sapphire stone.
the speck of peace
to forget the existence,
and effects of this heartache,
and secret sin

enamored by her beauty,
i allow the silent prayer of tranquility
to begin, and
like a sweet dialect
of a righteous fool,
the tip of
my tongue shouts out:

"serotonin.."
my sweet love,
come swiftly
and
blind my eyes before me
with your aroma where you belong

"serotonin.."
my sweet love,
can you carry this constant failure
that torments the air,
that i inhale,
the silent smoke
inside my lungs?

"serotonin.."
my sweet love,
can you carry this constant fear
inside my heart.
"serotonin.."
my sweet love;
"serotonin.."
my sweet love;
hurry swiftly
and
embrace
my soul.
sooth this anguish
heart..

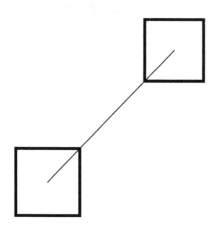

chaos and danger
were her first love
trauma and uncertainty
her parents

where do i fit in?
i don't

path of sin, stronger

it was his decision,
to forfeit
this frustration,
seeking forgiveness
on a mission to abandon
this illusion,
that he can't be loved,
fleeing, leaving
this path of sin,
believing that,
he did it for Him,
The One, above
his ultimate Best Friend
The Grand Master
The One, called,
"God," "Lord," "Jah,"
"Jehovah,"
the "El Elohim."

but, truthfully
ridiculously, and most
importantly,
pathetically,
he, did it all,
so that he,
could become
a brand new king, and
rekindle her love.

the type of love
that kept his eyes
focused, on the
love that only comes
from above,
and the visions of
a new hope,
future blessings
of what is to come

but,
by her lying to his face
she has no idea
what she has done..

she gave strength to the lone wolf
she he can endure the storm
much longer,
smiling through the rain,
and become one hundred times
more stronger,
rising out of the mud

by her truth,
by her lies,
she turned him into a man
who grows fonder of the rain,
impressed with the idea
of losing his breath

no longer feeling
the pain, of death
nor,
the tears flowing down from his eyes.

he has become the new king
of his own visionary world,
a leader,
a bleeder,
for those like him,
a born failure,
a seeder of the trees of truth,
his brothers,
his sisters,
freeing those bonded by humiliation,
alienation, rejection, & isolation
following the sting of heartbrea(kings)-
by rules of excommunication,
only to those who share his pain.

city moon,
los angeles

and there's nothing else
that i can say,
there's nothing else
that i can do,

that will prevent this rock of truth
from shining through
no, in the middle of the night
i lay awake,
my soul stares through the window
the sound of empty songs
the rain dancing
upon the window
still there's something in the way
because her earnest desires & pains
is something that i'll
forever recognize

because
under the glow of
this los angeles city moon,

there's no wind, and there's no light
there's no soul, and there's no fire
no hope, no tire
no fire shining bright
it's all inside our heads
it's all inside our minds.
but there is this
"something," in the way,
something preventing
this light of truth from you,
shining through
your sorrow
is nearly not the same
now there is nothing left to say?
there is nothing left to prove?
now i understand why
this key to our heart
no longer fits

and knives, flowers

he keeps playing with knives
because he enjoys the ride,
he loves the thrill
as he honestly feels
a chance to kill will enhance his life.
but he never can he ever,
seem to get it right?
so he endeavors
to keep playing with those knives
because he enjoys the ride,
he loves the thrill because,
he honestly feels,
a chance to kill will enhance his life.

no matter how dangerous
he will take the dive

because he will do what he wants
he will do what he pleases,
and he will do it again
until he gets what he needs.

he throws the knives in the air,
confident that he'll catch their glide,
but they crash down
and slash his body
self inflicting,
yet he feels victimized?

blames everyone but himself,
nor his blurry eyes?
because he will do what he wants
he will do what he pleases,
and he will do it again
until he gets what he needs

166

he picks the flowers
because he enjoys their colors,
pins them on the wall
for his selfish
observation,
but forgets
to feed
support
water
and nourish
until they die away
and float behind the curtains
and then into the fire
to burn away like
all the others

for a certain,
he will pluck more and more
for another journey in store,
because his heart
and mind becomes
more bored and torn

but there's no stopping him
he's a hidden narcissist

because he will do what he wants
he will do what he pleases,
and he will do it again
until he gets what he needs.

moon, midnight

the midnight moon cried out
and passionately said:

"dry your tears, and rise my son
i too, exist in darkness
and yet, i still shine alone
you can too.
if you put forth the effort,
if you do choose
to be,
happy."

no, i don't always enjoy
being alone,
but if my solitude,
silence
and
absence
will draw me closer to you,
then i suppose i will always endure it

no matter the agony
no matter the pain
no matter the cold
it will all be to my bones

for if the sun always rises
then i guess
i will always smile
no matter how murky
or how dark,
there is still beauty in the rain

i made a promise
to my friends asleep underground,
that we will
hold hands together again
when the last day arrives
this is why i keep going,
this is why i must remain strong
so that the stardust
that lies upon their graves
may shine
upon their heads
when they
rise

act v; scene: ii

"the angel of my nightmares"

enter: "failure, beauty, beast, insomnia, chocolate, alcohol,
rose, and angel.."

my nightmares,
angel of my

you will forever be an angel
in a sundress
dancing in that sweet midnight
october wind,

at least that is how i will
choose to,
remember you
but because
you are now existing, resting,
beneath this earth,
my desperate heart of stone
will never love again

so maybe it's too late
to regain sight of
all that we have lost and
now have found

so i've got to hold on to all these moments

no,
i won't let them go,
or, maybe it's too late
for redemption now?
just like the blanket of
pale white snow
across
the streets tonight,
from this doll house
full of
open wounds
i hope to one day,
whiten out
my sins against you

171

and the stained glass lights
from this church next door,
casts its luminous lights
bursting in this room
reminds me of
your heavenly eyes,
that used to shine,
as bright as the northern lights
without a pause in time,
under this northern sky,

a place where the
proposal was set,
but never began

for the demand to be loved
is in fact,
the greatest arrogance
and now,
i could never make you
love me again,

because when all is lost
something else is found

and when
all else fails,
love can never fail..

but did i fail you?

or will you fail me too?

because there is nothing that,
i would not do
if it means that i could
remain close to you,
and wake up next to you
but,
you give me nothing to hold on to

but i fear it is too late
to keep you, the only one
i love
from giving up on me?

and i guess it's too late
for forgiveness?

may Jah forgive me

and maybe it's
too late to make
your family mine?
too late,
to wake up,
to our children
near the ocean shore?
too late
to hold each other
under this moonlight galore?

everything reminds me of you

yes, everything
reminds
me
of
you

for you will
forever be my angel,
in a sundress
and
my
desperate,
ambitious
heart will never
love again

kiss, her final

her kiss was
the most painful,
for the simple fact,
that i knew that i,
a monster,
would never kiss them again

it was like kissing fine rose petals
a day after,
their final exposure
from the morning dawn's soft rain
her aroma
so memorizing,
so splendid,
so traumatic,
that losing her
became my greatest pain,
my greatest pleasure
my greatest failure

but holding her,
but smelling her,
became the world's greatest adventure

i miss her,
my heartbeat's greatest blister,
a disaster,
no cure for,
this
new
form
of
cancer

how could i,
a monster,
even
ever
begin to kiss another?

i simply wonder,
if this is what
hell feels like?

it must be,
for ultimately,
i am left to wonder,
suffer,
endure,
and
fight this fine plight
of
losing her
forever

come from, where did you

where did you come from?
like a drug, are you really
the only one, who
can make a strong man
like myself
feel this way?

where did you learn
that ability from?
with an aroma,
a fragrance, that'll trance
a righteous man's
heart astray?
like the glow of moonlight
on an ocean shore,
you gravitate my eyes
towards your-
picture
perfect
beauty,
that shines more
radiantly, than
one million suns

for this reason,
i don't think, that,
you know,

you're so beautiful..

it is this type of
rare beauty that
makes kings remove their crowns
drop to their knees,
begging for you not to leave

such an ability,
definitely, blows
my mind away
for your existence
is an unseen reality,

a presence felt,
that,
simply causes my thoughts
to bleed

did you know,
you have this kind of power
over kingdoms and worlds?
such a thought
consumes me,
confuses me,
that such a fine,
wonder
such as that of yourself
remains blind
behind,
your unintentional power

i don't think that you
even realize,
that it is this type of
rare beauty,
that
makes kings remove their crowns
drop to their knees,
begging for you not to leave

where did it all come from?
with a smile
and a heart that
can keep me hypnotized?

and a disappearance,
that'll strike
my heart to criticize
this air,
that i breathe
i forget to walk

you may be the only one..

with a heart
that can make me
the beast to your beauty,
with a mind
and a pair of eyes made of stars ,
that can start a riot
between kings to fight over
and a voice that can soothe,
any lost and forgotten child

that is why i cry for you
behind the scenes of my closed doors
as my body aches for you,
as i reach
for
this phone

i don't think that you
even realize,

that it is this type of
rare beauty
that
makes kings remove their crowns
drop to their knees,
begging for you not to leave.

beauty

in her story,
although
she was adored by many,
she was the only one
who was lost in the vanity
of her popularity
who was really the true beauty,
who was hidden in silence
alone.
lost in a town
who only adored her
physical beauty,
her eyes, her skin, her hair
she remained hurt,
saddened,
disappointed,
that no one stimulated
her mentally

not impressed
by outward hopes
on beauty,
secretly,
she hoped
to find a connection
with genuine and
impressive meaning

to her,
finding such a
connection,
would be easy,

if only she knew
that her true love,
was a man who
possessed a heartbeat,
that was quickly fleeting.
she saw the inside of
his mind,
the channel through
his soul,
everyone else saw
corruption
but she saw,
so
much more.

in the mirror,
he saw a monster
a beast,
for his demons were not dragons
or monsters,
but were a flask and a senate,
not to mention,
an abusive and alcoholic mother

but to her, he was the answer
but to her, he was the cure
he was no monster
he was the one,
who understood her pain

our love, the ghost of

our desperate hearts have led us astray
after bleeding, creating shapes
in different twists and shades

creating a new sensation within us

a thirst for the sunlight
a thirst for the dawn of day
we'd decline if we had nothing else

so we hold on,
we hold on..

even when this candle's burnt out
no we won't let this pain go,
because we are all afraid to hope
more comfortable, to let go
of something that has kept us alive
for so long, so strong

so we hold on,
we hold on..

because, we want it so bad
this one thing we can't have,
this one thing called "love"

beast

cursed by a condition
beyond his control,
a hidden monster,
who lives
hidden
within the broken
mirrors of his outward
appearance

he haunts the night
and dwells within
the solidarity shadows of
his unopened books,
and uninspired poetry
he cuddles the cold air
he welcomes the night
he is the monster
who ponders
about his future,
all alone.

hated and ignored
for what whisperers portray,
angry and resentful
he has become
to those who belittle him
and stay away.
they forgot who he was,
and focus on what he's become,
they evade from his face,
afraid of his curse
and hope he stays away,

they curse at his bitterness
and what he's become
as if their actions of gossip
weren't the reasons why
he turned out this way?

hopeless to forever abide
alone,
by this curse,
the real problem was
his sad and lonely
heart had no reason
to pump.
As the rose petals
of his fate
simply
glide away,
so was his desire
to find the only one
woman,
who will by his side
remain.
The beast within himself
began in his agony,
to complain,
that life is nothing more but
bitterness,
sadness,
loneliness
and
misunderstood **pain**

grow with this planet

heal the earth, heal yourself

rose, beautiful

the beautiful rose,
even when it
stands alone, is touched,
violated,
simply because of its *beauty*.
unwanted,
unwelcome,
unwillingly,
the hands of the evil decide
that it's purity shall blemish
by their disgusting
hands that thirst
to touch
and
contaminate
her petals

enduring the rain
the wind
the storm,
the thriving rose
becomes,
the evidence necessary
to warn, others
and advises that the
sun still shines
to keep the soul
warm.

nothing, and everything

when his heart was left all alone,
her maiden eyes
and imperfect hair,
made her heart
his home,
trapped
lost,
between
the sun,
the moon
the sky
his angel
taught his heart how to fly
alone

she
floats
above
his broken heart
asleep in the grave,
dancing upon the moonlight of love

alone,
forgotten,
afraid
if his sinful soul can be saved?

she reminds him of
the love that comes from above

that is why he will always hear her
voice when she calls his name
through her eyes that bleed cry,
guided by the tears of her eyes,
her lies
her anguish,
makes his heart scream inside

confused and alone?
why does this angel
of his nightmares
live on in his dreams?
in a place
more happy
than his heart has ever seen

lost between the sea and the sky
his angel taught his heart to fly
fly away,
on the lone branch
in his solitude,
there he finally
was able to greet the sunrise
and embrace
the bleeding moon

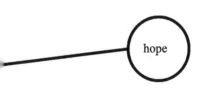

hope

breeze, ocean

i have waited almost forever,
to simply taste the exquisite pleasure
of having this affection
oh of what a joy it would be
having an angel like you
to become

my guidance
my direction
my protection

you are the reflection
of the universe,
the ultimate stimulation
the ultimate cosmic connection

oh if i could only
embrace the true warmth
from within your touch!
then i would truly
discover,
what my heart is now beating for
because your love is my oceanic breeze
where your aroma,
turns my nightmares
into the softest,
the most sweetest of all dreams,

to a place where your kiss
is the breath of life?
your touch,
your eyes,
my chance of heaven,
my hope for joy

oh what your absence
would definitely mean
what it could destroy

my hope for this reality
you my darling
are my tranquility
never leave me please
for you are my reason for peace
never flee, from me
and for eternity,
you shall be mine

my chance for hope,
my chance for family,
my chance for unity
and the rising of the sun?

oh my only beloved
you are the blood flow
within my veins,
the breath of life, that
flows from within my lungs
you are my romantic
whisper,

you are my greatest love

says, s(he)

her mouth says
"i love you,"
but her eyes say
"i hate you,"
her mouth says
"i hate you"
but her eyes say
"i love you."

what does her heart say?

how could it speak?
something so cold
so lifeless,
something that doesn't even   *((beat))*
what is this emotional test?

a level of *wo(man)tic*
romantic confusion,
a hopeless, desperate,
fueled by lust or love?
type of *illusion*
or blessing?

she is the dangerous type,
of woman,
because of her hidden scars,
she blindly pushes far away
these fallen men.

these fallen men who believe
that it is best to pretend
to be friends
in a place where you belong
if you're not in love with anyone
please remember to
stay where you are"

she is the *devil.*

the type of woman
who fools his heart,
into *believing*
that, he is,
someone special that
his heart is more worthy
of something on a greater level.
meaning, her

her eyes deliver a spell,
a convincing
that she is the one
who will love his heart forever.
however,
she the devil has
no intentions of loving him
she strikes now,
she kills him,
she delivers the final blow
she looks him in the eyes,
and says,
"let's just be fri(end)s"

skin, chocolate

in a world where "blackness,"
is associated with
"darkness,"
where "black" and "darkness"
has become associated,
with evil,
her skin and appearance
in my eyes,
has becomes
the greatest luxury
in the known universe.

her skin
yes,
her chocolate skin
not only represents her sweetness
her splendor
but represents also,
her strength and endurance
to which i crave

in a world that classifies her
as not beautiful
she walks outside,
to a world that praises
a polar opposite
for its ideological beauty

yet this woman
she smiles
she dances
and embraces the warm sun

her beauty,
yes,
her cosmic beauty,
becomes so inspiring,
that when i blink,
yes
even when i blink
i contaminate my eyes
with a darkness
that is everything else
but her

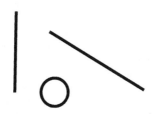

brown,
eyes
chocolate

brown eyes are beautiful,
and not just because.
for they remind us of
everything in
this world,
that keeps
us
secure
keeps us-
warm.
like
coffee,
chocolate,
dark chocolate;
they nourish the soul.
brown eyes are so *refreshing;*
telling the heart to please show us more.

absence, your

allow
your absence
to educate,
teach him, and them
that you are not someone
to take for granted.
you are not an option
you are plan a,

the only way

i and you,
        honeymoon

let us say our vows
let us escape
and never return
to this void called, "life."
let's leave our cell phones behind
our social media "likes"
"fri(end)s,"
and
never
ever
pretend,
that our love is a destination
that will someday end.

let's not go to paris
although we can,
let's not go to italy
although we can,
let's not go to africa
although we can,

instead,
let us go to our cabin
in the snow locked woods
where our true love can finally begin.
i and you,
our honeymoon,
i and you, my angel
forever,
to a place where the snow crystal roses
still openly bloom.

i want to chop us firewood
for the warmth of
our cabin home,
i want to roast the
same s'mores,
my grandmother made
for me in my childhood.

i want to lay in the snow with you,
no matter how old, or how
cold we are,
for my purpose,
is to chill your skin
so i can
bring you back in
to our
cabin house room
and then
warm you with the chocolate
of my skin

i want to read to you
the sonnets of my
upcoming books
whilst i watch and look
on your face,
as i play with
your imperfect hair.
do i dare,
mention,
the thoughts inside of my mind?
you already know them,
every secret
every inclination
of my soul,
you already know the secret to.

after our night of
cosmic intimacy,
where the stars of the universe
flow through our minds,
i want to wake up next to you,
taking this chance,
to catch a glimpse
of what forever feels like
by gazing into your eyes

i want to carry you downstairs
there,
our breakfast
will not be food,
but will be a prayer,
to our God,
giving him thanks
for blessing us for each other

but in actuality,
the reality is
that my prayer,
will be the same prayer
that i was wishing for
throughout my entire life.
when i look into your eyes,
i do not see a woman
i see the healing of
my pain
the family i always wished for
the joy i always dreamed of
the ultimate hope of finally
erasing
my alienation,
my humiliation,
my orphaned heart.

solitude,
sweet

like a bird that cannot
flap its wings
i alone am left
without you,
the sadness
in my heart,
has withered away my spirit,
yes my passion of fire
has become
just like smoke..
from the roof of my home
the stars above,
have become my
only association
my friends
my family
are nowhere to lift me up?

love?
support?
teamwork?
such concepts makes my heart
chuckle, then feel sick
the only kinship,
the only fri(end)ship,
the only meaningful connection
is the voice of solitude
my only beloved.
the voice speaks to me,
like a wise mentor to a young man
like a maiden embracing
her long lost friend,
solitude and her warmth
are the blanket
that warms
then softens
my heart of stone
covered in the snow.

for you, new

if i surrendered my bleeding heart
into His open hand,
hopefully,
He will grasp it firmly,
and *never let go..*

His creation will always
be my favorite instrument
of His love
when i hear the ocean,
which is the sound of His voice
so tranquil
like angelic voices singing as one.
my urge to confess my love to Him,
held back,
like sweet secrets,
held under the tongue.

i would cry forever,
if i lost the beauty of His hands
i will always be a victim
haunted by this flesh
as i fail each and every test
for i am not
the greatest man
because my heart will fly,
fly into the darkness
under this truth:
that i need to be made new
new for you.

i would rather spend,
my entire life in solitude,
ultimate loneliness
instead of breathing
this earth,
without you

if that would mean
i could defend your Holiness
so that you
will forever dwell, receive
the love that you deserve,
because you do exist

my love,
your love is more soothing
than the waves over my shoulders
upon the ocean's shore
and every time i feel defeated,
i only thirst for you more
if virtue,
and the sufferings of the heart
were something
that i did not know,
our love for each other
would exist in the form
of eternal tear drops,
sent from the sky
wasted upon floor

my life was a shadow

until i knew,
that my sorrows, sadness,
and shame,
would be wiped completely,
just from knowing your Name

i will always
remember your love,
and you are forever,
everything changes,
everything will be made new
my Father,
my Friend,
i will make myself
new for you.

4:04pm

if there ever existed,
an ocean made of tears
my darling i'd own it,
dwell in its possession
forever
because
the truth is:
you wouldn't believe it,
my love,
they would all be
made from my own eyes
and heart
that is now as blue
as sapphire stone

if i had a choice
between life without you
forever
or death by torture,
my love,
i'd rather
choose the latter ,
if it meant that
i can still hold you
inside of my arms
beneath the graves of forever
i am haunted by
the mere thoughts of you
and how we met

when you first
texted me at 4:04pm,
when i asked
my dearest friend,
to persuade you into,
giving me a helping hand
in school

when you walked over
when our very
virgin
fiery
eyes
first blindly connected
instinctively
passionately
instantly
i thought about,
what our first kiss
would eventually feel like
all those memories,
continue to fold
inside of my heart,
the tranquility
of smelling one thousand roses,
every time i play with your hair.

can you understand?

or begin to even comprehend
the amount and level
of agony, of pain,
that stems
from each beat
of my fragile heart?
the feeling of loss,
when i am no longer
grasping your tender hand?

for without you,
i am lost,
helpless, half dead inside
desperate, cold
and out of breath

south from the north

i love you
oh my darling,
please do not leave me!
for if you do,

i will never love again

do wake me up with your presence
which is the width of your fingers
the heaven of your body
with your hair
with your eyes!

yes,

oh my only beloved
please make my heart beat
once again,
with your smile
which is as powerful as the wind
that blows south from the north

what then, is it
that a desperate man
like that of myself
ever ask for?

it is the hope in your eyes
and the fire
beneath your tongue
to help defeat this dragon
which is the faith that you will return
but my dark darling,
it is not the truth

insomnia

in its purest form,
insomnia
becomes more pleasant
than the nightmares
and visions
of you

the fear of sleeping
within
the slumbers of my unrest
exist,
because in its dreams
you are happy,

but
in reality,
you are not here.

the choice and decision,
between sleep,
or insomnia forever,
i would rather,
choose the latter,
for
it is the only way,
the **nightmares**
which are the hopes
of you and i,
may finally be gone *forever*.

last, last snowflake
  by the,
    marriage proposal

on the arctic carpet,
one knee shall bend
for her,
and look within
the pupil of her
eyes of fire
inflamed,
the chilling air
locked within my lungs
shall say:

"my darling sweet november star,
let us walk forever together,
through the hills
of infinite wisdom,
growth and power.
oh, *my only beloved,*
will you forgive me now
for all my future errors,
if it meant for now,
that only i,
can hold your tender hand
and kiss you upon
your lips forever?"

the greatest pleasure in my life,
is to make you smile
my endeavor
is to surrender
my pride,
just in order
to hear
your honest laughter

the fragrance
the aroma
of your body
and the nectar
from your lips,
the sweetest splendor?

oh,
my sweet dosage,
of serotonin
and euphoria
combined
you are my serenity,
you are my tranquility
you are my war,
you are my devastation
without question,
will you love me?
will you marry me?
please be mine
forever
oh,
my only true friend.

i hope that someday, you will see, that your absence somehow gave me life

then i could finally and truly, take my first breath
if only i could play with your imperfect hair again,

again,
in my dreams

when i believe,
that i am finally free,
no longer chained
by the hopes
and aspirations of us,
you and i,
when i believe that i can
spread my wings
soar, and fly
away to safety,
my heart begins to beat,
once again but fragile

when i encounter my dreams of you,
how can something
so splendid, so sweet as sleep
remain so tragic?
like magic
like a curse
you arise once again,
inside my dreams,
your ocean, blue eyes
so vivid, so horrific,
my beloved friend,
the only one i adore
to which i am chained,
bonded, imprisoned by
your absent love.

in my dreams once again,
only there you exist,
only there you breathe
when in reality,
you are absent
and continue, to, make
my heart and
thoughts bleed.

my hope,
my ambition,
my motivation,
my inspiration,
becomes faint like a last breath,
a heartbreaking evaporation.

which is-
my experience,
within,
the end of our undying
friendship.
this agonizing torture,
this unbearable desperation,
prolongs my pain,
without you by my side,
i awake in tears
without you,
next to me,
all of my fears exist,
when you persist,
in my dreams again

please go away

my angel,
my beloved
my best friend,

my angel of my nightmares,

you drop me
down to the knees of
my reality,
oh my darling,
you give me life,
even when i cannot breathe

drug, like a

your eyes
are like a **drug**
that i
just can't quit

i stare through
their glory,
as my heart grows
faint, sick,
knowing that,
i can never have you

you are my
personal obsession,
my own dose of
heroin(**e**),
a feeling,
a vibe,
that i just can't kick ?
in my sheets
at night
when
i
am
all
alone,

there is a vibration
a pain,
an unknown emptiness
bouncing within my bones
thrown about on the floor
reaching for my phone,
i know
that something is wrong

i need my dose,
my hit,
i need this sensation
the joy
that i just can't quit?

your kiss is,
the thin needle
that hits my veins
your aroma
your presence,
the cure
that erases my silent pains?

the agony!
of not having your touch
the *humiliation*
knowing,
that this,
that this,
that *this*,
is
all
my fault

finally found you,
have i

have i finally found you?
my sweet oceanic,
wind breeze?
so gentle,
so soft,
that i hope to never
be of loss to
your scent,
your aroma
oh,
my angelic whisper
the tranquil sound
that
transforms my
nightmares,
into the sweetest
of dreams
stay with me,
please,
let
us
even,
die together

but have i,
already lost you?
the remedy to
my pain?
now, i am
a foolish
desperate man,

who cannot speak
lost within the darkness
of my tears

oh my angelic whisper,
please speak
once more for me
and allow
these dreams
of your silent
absence flee from me

do come back,
and
embrace me with your
holy love,
for your existence
is the reflection,
of the divine love
that comes from above

i am like a mouse
on the ledge of a wall
contemplating this thing called "life"
and i no longer have the desire
to look for a place
called "home"
for no home, is home
without your touch
to keep me warm

a woman with a plan is a goddess

act v, scene i

"dawn of the night "

enter: the nightlife, intoxication, confessions,
moons, stars, and crisp cold air..

light, red

by the flash
of her eyes,
and
the nectar of her lips,
i know,
that she wants to
stay together,
but by the heat
of her mouth,
the twists,
between our tongues,

i don't think that i can

by the structure
of her eyes
their shape,
or quite simply, by
the style she creates,
combs her hair, or
quite passionately,
by the way
she chooses to smile, or
the way she inhales
this air

i **know** what you are

you are a red light,
the "type,"
who is not so sure
if you can make this 'thing'
between you and him
"official"

even when you two
had a great night,
you aren't the type
to text
and say that-
"i miss you"

oh, no
he doesn't know,
that you possess
a cold soul,
a heart of stone,
that can make it easy,
leaving,
after smiling all
night long

assuming
that his intentions
are wrong,
you decide that
he's deceiving,
making you believe,
that, you are
just another girl
locked,
behind the texts
within his phone

even though you need him
like he needs you,

but
you aren't the type
to admit the fact
that your black heart
is incapable
for them to love

because
your young life,
reflects strife,
failure,
defeat,
rejection,
i can see it in the
structure your eyes

when you watch
the people you want,
the people you love,
walk the other direction,

you have no choice
but to become numb-
to the chase,
for your own heartbeat's
sake and protection

identical, the

they are all identical,
the same
dancing nightclubs
house parties
tight, **black** spandex,
black neck chokers
thick, shiny make up,
and
afraid of the rains

their hearts are engulfed,
troubled,
by the flames,
of their fornication,
regret and shame,
that is why they all,
are out **tonight**
in order to
escape from their hidden pains
and are out to gain,
something "better"

they are all so afraid,
ashamed,
by their troubled hearts
hidden sins,
and guilty consciences

yet
find joy down the dark streets
filled with danger,
crime,
broken hearts
drunken mysteries
and then,
becoming forced upon

their weekends are necessary,
are essential
because in their
young lives,
they,
simply have nothing **better to
do.**

fully prepared,
to dance their hidden pains away
to get their thoughts
off that one
lost soul,
who is male,
who just can't
escape their mind
from his,
sick,
twisted
controlling methods
of persuasion
manipulative words
empty love
cunning intellect
smile
laughter, and
his way of making her feel
special

they are all identical,
the same,
adjusted only, to the fame

for no one,
gentlemen
will love or adore you
like she used to

so now that she's gone
never show the universe
how alone,
how cold,
how numb,
you've become
because of the absence
of her static,
that makes your heart beat,
then bleed,
heed this warning,
flee, retreat, and give up,
this pursuit,
this quest
this journey
this pain,
called, "love"

for it is a reality unseen,
something,
that you'll never again
reach, receive, achieve
nor even believe
indiscriminately

now when it is all said and done,

i myself have fought
through the journey of love,
lived long enough,
and discovered,
we were all better off,
dissolving this thing called, "love,"
and now that,
although i am young
i too have,
survived through the
pain of heartbreaking
love

i prefer to let it
all end up,
by letting it
burn itself away
so now i've closed my lungs,
so i don't inhale this smoke
i took the plunge,
dove,
deep into the ocean of hurt
i let it all burn up
realizing,
that i was never loved,
realizing
that i am not "the one

yet,
she still
deserves to be loved
and
i deserve,

to end up all by myself.

i have exposed my wrongs
i adored my evil, now,
it is all too late,
to remain hopeful, of
changing my ways,
so i did my part
because,
i couldn't behave,
but what does it matter?

for they all feel, and
breathe the same

what do i do
when i continue,
to antagonize, abuse
her inner heart bruise,
for my amusement?

when i intoxicate our love?
when she still wants to stay
but, oh?
how can i leave?
when they all feel the same

i want to burn it all up,
but the ashes of my hurt,
my lust remain
she collects hopes of us,
a good man returning
and attempting
to regain his good ways

and now she has gotten away
nor will you take the chance,
to play the game
because all of the
other ones are-
only addicted to your **"Social Fame"**
for they all look the same to you,
now that she is gone
look forever forward,
to what will definitely never come

another smile,
another sunset
another failure
another regret

another chance at hurt
and heartbreak,
that will shake your bones,
leaving you all alone..
and, make you,

dwell upon her absent love
forever

night, lovers of the

text messages, phone calls
instagram scrolling,
makeup, high heels, pretty women
nothing but distractions

everyone's heart is out tonight,
searching for that [*something*]
i zone out and
all i want indeed, is
peace of mind
and a little moonlight hunting,

2 am,
street tacos
coffee highs and lows
are we stopping?
plane tickets
travel expenses
and the future regrets
come home knocking

all this "love"
and her insecurities
are the reason,
all the "affection"
and the aim-
to cure her *pain*
was the central problem
and the *reason*
all the "attention"
was the mission
for her *completion*
that's her secret motive
with our hearts
beating to the ground
i better slow it down
or she'll be *heartbroken* in the morning

art, the perfect

for them their home
was a place of where,
people love, and come and go
so, they perfected the art
of being alone
became a pro
of holding on,
then
painfully letting go

and when they say
that they just don't.
"feel-the-same."

it is because their heart
has had enough,
of all the lies
and all of
the wicked,
twisted,
perverted
ungodly games

and when they say,
"let's just be friends"
some know-the-pain?
it is
the feelings of rejection,
the feelings of losing
every-single-day,

those that never *ever*
seem to loyally stay?
are the ones who
are quick to say
those three little words

then their trust becomes betrayed

and i suppose
she had no idea
how her love
was a power that
could persuade me,
to believe that
that my honesty
was never enough
to break free from these
feelings of our romantic
inadequacies

so many ways
so many places
that our love could go
but she too, was the
type to never hold on,
she was a pro
of holding on,
then painfully letting go
but she could never know,
how my heart beats
when i am all alone,

it beats better,

without her aroma
disrupting the blood flow
within my heart of stone,
nullifying the arctic sensation,
the chilling of my
flesh, my bones
as if they're covered
within the snow,
and when,
it comes to her species
oh, do i
love it when they come and go

day, new year's

the october, autumn twilight
many unspoken words
hidden underneath
our breaths,

yes,
i've had dreams of
this newly found redemption,
in combination with a mixture,
a wine glass full
of my sinful regrets

and
insight of the beauty
behind this bleeding red horizon,
amongst one of many murky rains
locked within the clouds of this pain,
i could hear your voice
but
i no longer could scream
your name

oh,
if only i could
make you see,
that your last breath solely
belonged to me

then i would take back
all the painful
things i've said on our
last new year's eve

so let us drink to *forgiveness,*
let us drink to *our regrets,*
let us drink to the ones
we have loved and lost,
let us never forget,

228

the never ending circle of our pain,
for the fallen petals of lust and love,
were the only treasures to gain
let us drink for
being only human
for
that is,
this imperfection,
it is the reason
of our beauty,
for
the biggest sin,
is that we
are
all too human

too human, for
trying to
love ourselves again

hunt, prowl

shout out my name
my darling
when you are afraid
when times get rough
when you are angry

and like a lion
that rushes to fight for the kill
i will fight for you
if that means i can hold you forever
if it means that i can kiss you
endlessly

since the last time
i laid my eyes on you
i forgot what family felt like
even though we have been through hell
i have come to understand,
that you belong to me
and i,
to you

alone, when i am

i have something to address
to you,
but i don't know how
i will say this,
but my darling, i guess,
i will try my best
to confess,
to express,
and only say
one thing

that i failed this test again,
that i've given into sin,
that i've been evil again
yes,
i've been unfaithful to you,
but more importantly
unfaithful to Him

because
with this type of mind
along comes heightened gifts
yet what's frightening,
these heightened gift
brings treasures
as well as illusions
and,
those illusions
when i'm intoxicated
begin to take over
and force me to take
one more sip,
so that i can slip away
this pain,
so that i can forget again,
what it means
to lose a beloved friend

231

when i'm under this influence
i also then try my best,
to forget who i am,
and
forget what
you mean to me
forget the feeling that,
even after all this time,
that you
still
mean
the
world
to
me

so when,
i-am-alone,
the thoughts of us resurface,
and i want you to know,
that behind these closed doors,
my body is itching for you
as i reach for this phone
now i know,
that
my love for you
is only circumstantial

that i only want you when,
i-am-alone
that i only thirst for you when,
i-am-alone
that my heart beats for you when,
i-am-alone
that my soul thrives for you when,
i-am-alone

it's not fair
for you to begin
to love this man again.
for this man again is
no longer who i am.
for i have failed you
multiple times over
and tried to win,
this battle over this flesh,
this sin

this heart breaking battle within
and against,
these hidden sins
yet again and again,
i fall for you
in the end

stay away from me my darling

for i understand,
that i am indeed

a

cunning,
desperate,
and manipulative man,
for my thoughts,
actions,
admiration,
and love for you
is completely illogical,
incompletely circumstantial
for this man
only wants you
when,
he-is-alone

that
he only thirsts for you
when,
he-is-alone

that
this heart beats for you
when,
he-is-alone

that
this soul thrives for you
when,
he-is-alone

"you are not alone."

"you are not alone"
and yet,
when s(he) speaks,
no one
listens,
and
when s(he) cries,
s(he)
wipes tears,
in the dark,
and
when s(he) needs family,
s(he)
scrolls through the
social media feed
and
watches you and your kinsfolk
frolic
as s(he) picks the thorns
from off
of (h)er(is)
tongue.

for you, new
pt II

if i surrendered my bleeding heart
into her open hand,
hopefully
she will grasp it firmly,
and,
never let go..

her love and misery
will be my favorite instrument
of her love,
the simple sound of her voice,
so tranquil
like angelic voices singing as one.
my urge to confess my love
to her,
held back
like sweet secrets,
held under the tongue..

i would cry forever,
if, i lost the beauty of her eyes.

i will,
always be a victim,
of the illusions
of she and i,

because my heart will fly,
fly into the darkness
under this truth:
that i need to be made new,
new for you
new like a fallen snowflake
new like a rising moon

i would, rather spend,
my entire life
in solitude,
ultimate, loneliness,
rather,
than
without you,
for you,
if that would mean,
i could defend, your holiness,
so that you,
will forever dwell, in happiness

my love,

your love is more soothing
than the waves over my shoulders
upon the ocean's shore
and
every time i feel defeated,
i fail,
i only thirst for you more,

if virtue,
and the sufferings of the heart,
were something that i did not know,
our love for each other
would exist in the form
of bleeding tear drops,
sent from the sky,
wasted upon floor

my life was a shadow,

until i knew,
that my sorrows, sadness,
and cryings for an angel,
would be wiped completely,
just from knowing you

237

i stand helpless
defenseless, desperate,
while i stare deep
into your eyes,
knowing that forever,
will be a time,
that you and i,
will fly,
fly into the darkness
under this new
truth:
that we both,
she and i
will both, be made new
new for You

i will,
always
remember your love,
and your love,
everything changes,
everything will be made new
my darling,
my love

i will make myself
new for you.

fragrance, guilty

put down your perfume,
and surrender
to the flash
of my
eyes.
yes,
become addicted
to this illusion,
this intimacy
between
you and i,

this is false love,

this is false love.
like the night sky before us,
let me deceive you,
with the shadows
of my broken
heart

i'm so wrong
i'm so wrong

to let you in my heart
to let you in my heart

grab my book
from off
your shelf,
read to me your happiest line
as i listen, i will ponder
that you deserve
to be loved,
and
i deserve to be by myself

scars and wounds

my darling i do not
blame you,
for being so true,
for being so beautiful,
for being so unique,
exquisite,
with a simplistic smile,
that makes kings
start believing,
that your magic
is meant for some type
of cure?

i am a fish to your pond,
your aroma becomes
my hook into your mind
your eyes, the perfect lure
your touch, the automatic cure,
to my fleeting heart,

because when i smile
through the eyes of other women
oh, i only
dwell upon the thoughts
of me and you
and it's true,
when you go out on "dates,"
even though you resent me,
you wish that you,
were here with me too

this is why i do not want
anyone else but you, to
heal my scars and wounds
i desire no one else but me,
kissing, you softly
honestly, passionately,
satisfyingly, caressing,
and
pleasing your appealing body

i will not accept the pain
in my chest
when i witness you,
angelically
glowing in that white dress,
standing there, yet,
next to another man
such a nightmare!

all of my friends
and enemies,
want to know
why my heart will not beat
why i shiver, shake,
from your absence
why my feet cannot move,
but i don't stress over it,

because with your pretty eyes
and smile,
i forget to walk,
with
your fragrance
and glow of your skin,
oh i continuously
forget who,
and
what i am

this is why i do not
want
anyone else
but you,
to
heal my scars, and wounds,

i desire no one else
but me,
kissing you softly
honestly, passionately,
satisfyingly, caressing,
and
pleasing your appealing body

water, fire in the

love is the sweetest feeling
when you have the ability
to openly believe in it
like fire in the water
the burning sensation between us
must produce a trail that ends like smoke

when you are open
when you are exposed

even the origin of all creation
have had their turn to figure it all out

fire in the water
fire in the water
is the body of our love

fire in the water
fire in the water
is force that keeps us stable

like a sociopath
stabilizes their hands around a neck

monsters

it is a
bittersweet truth, that
must be said, that
monsters
aren't hidden
in the dark
locked,
under
our beds

but
to catch them,
you must first take
a closer look nearby,
instead for the
monsters are buried
down deep,
inside the
caskets of our heads

deep,
so deep,
into the darkness
is where some of us hide,
monsters are real
they are given birth,
inside the caskets of our minds
they are critical,
not magical,
or imaginative
if you weren't too sure
about yourself,
now you know,

you can spot them
anywhere
it is no miracle

be watchful of their
horror,
be watchful of their
terror,
be watchful of their
allure
they are cunning
they are oh,
so terrible

watch out for even their laughter

they are not in forests,
rivers or mountains,
real monsters are found
lost,
floating,
reflecting
in
the mirror

vision, justice

i am vision,
i am justice,
i never thought that i could love
living in shadows,
fading away my existence,
life was never good enough.
but,
within the darkness,
of my own,
fragile,
and
desperate heart,
your eyes were the light
that shined my way

in a world trapped in violence,

through your eyes,
i wanted to be the man
who could save the day.

so, i said,
"i'm there for you."
no matter what.
"i'm there for you."
together,
never giving up.
you'll know when
it's true,
for you were there for me,
and i swear,
that i'll be there,
for you.

someone has changed me,
something has saved me,
now this is
who i am,

245

although i was blinded,
my heart did let me find that,
truth and honesty,
will bring humiliation
and pain
but will also
bring,
forth
a better man.

i didn't know that
you were always
in front of me?
life's mask of silence,
when i was cold and alone,
you were the only one,
who continued to,
believe in me.

within the darkness
within the hatred
your eyes were the light,
that shined my way

in a world trapped in violence,

through your eyes,
i wanted to be,
that man,
who can brighten everyone's day.

stone, heart of

can you keep a secret?
for how long,
while you hold
your innocent hand
above
the glass jar
of these,
cold & broken flames?

darling, you are a shipwreck
and i possess a heart of stone

all the wasted tears
i could dry
a river
for you
with my heart of stone
with your heart of stone

i can finally breathe,
i can finally breathe,
fire
water

i can finally breathe,
fire
i can finally breathe,
water

but only,
when you are
here, with me
you give me, the ability
to do such things!
but, you are not here,
in this seemingly reality
can i pry your fingers
away from everything,
i say and do?

and i just cannot forget you
with your heart of stone

i can finally breathe,
fire
i can finally breathe,
water
i can finally breathe,
fire
i can finally breathe,
water

when you are here
next to me,
but you are not here
with me,

where is my breath?
where is my only beloved?

only you
give me the will to exist,
you give me the will
this power,
to persist in this agony
which is the
absence of you,
hopefully,
you will return,
and
if not?
oh, i wish, that
this
pain will continue
for it is through
this pain,
that i dream upon
the very thoughts
of you
which is better than nothing at all

thank you

contanct me:
devonhewett@gmail.com
on instagram
hewett.vision

for questions/signed copies

"Fire in the Water"

Chapter 5

"The Voice of Confusion."

sample

of my upcoming novel

2018

"What is it Edmond?"

I actually ponder if admitting my feelings to Ana at this point were advantageous enough for me to mention. If it would be of any benefit to explain myself, I would gladly do so. An explanation however, on how my soul remains constantly on fire, troubled by the unknown mysteries of my past, is sure to be in vain. If I do mention word of, I would absolutely feel that I am babbling on again about something that I could not change; and a reality that Ana could never possibly perceive.

Do I dare mention about my tormenting experience with the young girl at the deli shop? I ponder if I should even express myself towards Ana about her; for I did not want to crush any of Ana's feelings if they still lingered around.

But what did it matter?

What did it matter to me if I did crush Ana's lingering feelings? I suppose that my thirst to become more of a courteous fellow, was an endeavor so strong, that I was willing to hide what I feel inside in order to succeed in becoming such.

Becoming a more courteous fellow, I suppose, was a challenge most exhausting for the central reason that hiding what I feel inside, although a daily practice, feels I am holding my breath under water.

It is almost impossible.

"So..are you going to tell me?" She pushed.

Ana, you are such a persistent soul.

I surrender to her pushy requests, and decide to only mention what was most troubling on my heart. Between my past, my present and my future, I decide to talk to Ana about the young girl whose name is apparently "September."

But, before I can move forward in this conversation of confession, Ana interrupts me with a surprising, and yet a shocking unprecedented question:

"Are you having, women problems?"

I freeze.

I am frozen in shock that she was clever enough to discern. But how did she know? Is she gifted in clairvoyance as well? Maybe I am not the only one who has the gift.

"Yes." I confessed, as she sighed deeply.

The look on her face appeared frightened. Like the face of someone who just had a stroke or the face of someone who had just seen a ghost. To my astonishment, the appearance made her slightly attractive to me for a split second. For it was the face of a woman, whose concern and care for me, was disappointed, only because..she was in love with me.

"Oh." she quivered.

She was disappointed.

"Ok, tell me then, wassup? Do I know this mystery girl? What is it about her exactly that is bothering you?"

I wanted to tell Ana that this woman makes me afraid. That I do not know who she is, and yet, every time I see her eyes, I am overwhelmed with guilt, shame, and at the same time, overwhelmed with unspeakable inspiration. But, I could not tell Ana that exactly. So, I softened the truth, in order to draw out how Ana might feel about this dilemma of mine, and how she feels about me..

"She makes me nervous." I tell her. "It is almost as if, she can read my thoughts and inclinations. It is not what she looks like, or what she says that makes me nervous.." I close my eyes, dramatically turning my face heavenward.

"Then what is it Edmond?"

"It is the way she looks at me that paralyzes me so."

"Oh.." Ana says again. But this time, it sprang from a hint of anger, jealousy, and a bit of sadness. What confirmed this was what Ana said next.

"Ya' know, she must be a really pretty girl if you feel this way for her by just looking at her. I mean, really, you don't know who she is, and yet you feel so strongly about her. So strong, that you are willing to ignore your friend's phone calls, even mine..so that you can travel to the mountains and be alone..? So that you can..think...about..her? Do I know her? What does she look like? She must be pretty."

She throws a handful of snow across the valley.

And it was at this moment, I realized that I lost this conversation.

Last year, Ana confessed her feelings for me. She told me that she feels strong in affection towards me because I make her feel safe; that I make her feel secure. I blame myself of course, for her affection and attraction, because I was indeed at fault for allowing her to feel this way. I blame the fact that I gave her my listening ear during all the time we spent our friendship together alone on this mountain.

252

Because of this, I well knew that it would be difficult to express myself fully about what is going on inside my mind in relation to *another girl.*

Ana was the *wrong person* to open up to about this mystery girl. Only because, she harbored feelings and a resentment. Resentment for the fact that I did not reciprocate romantic interest; even after all of her endeavors.

It was not much help either to be in an environment such as where we were in this moment; alone together, on a massive boulder viewing the enormous mountainous landscape covered in snow and awe inspiring beauty. A beautiful, and desolate place where Ana and I bonded over. The mountains, the trees, the angelic snowfall.. all of it, was a bad mixture of romantic ingredients, which its complex disturbed the atmosphere with a romantic glow.

"Ana, it is not that at all. The main reason why I feel so strong emotionally about this girl is because I believe-"

Before I could finish, I remembered that what I really wanted to say next would not be proper to voice. Ana simply would not understand what I would mean, and even if she did, I feel that I would be babbling on about what I could not change.

Oh how I wanted to say, that the central reason why I feel so strong about this mystery girl is particularly because I honestly feel that perhaps.. perhaps I know of her from somewhere, and that she knows who I am.

Perhaps, I know her from my forgotten past? Perhaps she knows who I am? Perhaps 'this' and perhaps 'that,' all of which became the fuel to the fire burning inside of me to solve this tormenting riddle.

This craving for knowledge and answers about my identity, propels my interest further because she might be a clue, unlocking a treasurable discovery. She has this astonishing beauty about her. Light makeup, large pupils, and a smile that competes with the glow of moonlight, is a combination indeed sure to grasp my attention and fuel this craving.

Like the appearance of an angel, she possesses a purity that I have not witnessed outside of my dreams. She seems fragile, vulnerable, and yet, has so much control over my composure. There are many factors that play into this game of wonder that make me feel paralyzed with curiosity when I even think about her. So, instead, I deflect from the issue, by softening my answers to Ana.

"Believe what-?" Ana impatiently persisted

"-believe that .."

I pause.

"Yes..?"

I sit still.

"Go on…"

I continue to pause unbearably.

Am I lost without words to fill in? Yes I am indeed. Perhaps the simple thought of this maiden freezes me in my tracks. I was perplexed during this agonizing interrogation, not to mention, that I was getting tired of lying. With no words coming forth from my lips, Ana decided to interfere with my composing of words-

"I find it funny that you absolutely do not share any feelings for me at all? That even though I have known you for a few years..and opened up all of my secrets to you.. you still don't care about me..and, you seem to be in love with a stranger. I don't know."

Due to her incriminating, I continue to pause.

"It's just unfortunate, that you.. you, of all men would fall for a woman just because? It does not make any sense to me at all. You never approach women, or express any interests towards anyone. She must be really something amazing ya know.. I guess someone more amazing than me I guess. I don't know.."

I was beginning to sense doubt and insecurity within Ana; I had to rush in. But only then, could I find a few comforting words to say-

"You are a thousand times more lovelier than stars of heaven, Ana. No doubt, you are already aware of that very fact. Do not allow my confusion, and stubbornness undermine your confidence.." I croaked in order to plead my case. To add harmony and sincerity, I was forced to follow that statement with a charming smile. A smile, that I am aware is able to calm a storm inside the women I inadvertently upset.

"I guess..I am not used to rejection.." She mumbled, biting her lip and turning her head to the left, deflecting my attention towards her soft brown eyes. Her neck exposed, and her perfume most delightful.

But how true her words were. Ana was not a woman who was used to rejection. Rejection, meaning *rejection from men*. Ana had such a soft and warm appeal to her beauty that nearly any man that caught sight of her, thirsted for her instantly. She had no trouble successfully attracting men.

She was so successful at attracting the opposite sex, that there was a high probability that whomever she adored, would adore her back; simply because.. she was, beautiful. It was easy for Ana. Saying that her success for romance was something as simple as taking candy from a baby would be an understatement. She explored the world of romance and it's drama to her heart's content. Her romance and affairs would swiftly end when the thrill was over, or when she got..bored.

I know this to be a fact for the simple reason that I was a witness to it all. Whether Ana and I were at the library, the mall, the park, or at a restaurant, she was always approached by a man. No matter how many men endeavored to claim her hand, she was no desperate fool. She knew that most men who approached her by responding to her beauty, were also responding to some other stimulus.

For she was aware, that they were out on quest, not for her heart, but were out on a quest for what she might be able to offer within the bedroom.

How uncivil..

Unfortunately as true as it may be, Ana did in fact have a strong sex appeal to her as well. Her body was slender, but without compromising her woman curvature. She exercised daily, and because of her vegetarian diet and healthy lifestyle, she retained a youthful glow; always appearing to look younger than her age. She was 24, and always passing for 17.

"You know Edmond, I guess it's not fair to expect you to share the same feelings that I do have for you." She lamented, but this time, turning her head around to face me. Her crystal, brownish, yellow eyes flashing deep into mine.

I found it amusing that when her eyes flash at me, I feel nothing at all. However, when the girl behind the counter flashes her eyes at me, I feel the most anxiety and perplexion.

"I guess I am a bit disappointed, for I never really have shared my secrets with any man; but I have shared them all with you, Edmond."

"Yes I know."

"I don't know, I guess I am just confused and disappointed. I thought, well, perhaps if I found you here, that maybe you would be thinking about us. So, when you told me that you thought about me..I felt a little excited that maybe you came around, and had a change of heart?"

I forgot that I said I was thinking about her while up here.

She continued -

"..so then, when I heard you speak about another girl, I felt a bit..sad."

"I feel absolutely horrible for toying with your expectations, Ana. I did not mean to.. I was not thinking clearly about what I was saying. It is just..that, I came up here to clear my thoughts and be alone. I did not intend for you to go out of your way looking for me, and then disappoint you..I am terribly sorry."

"You don't suppose that you can explain why, explain to me why.. you do not have feelings for me...but you feel that you share feelings with, her?"

In my defense, I sat up on the rock and wrapped my arms around my legs in a fetal position.

"I don't want to talk about it."

"Well you are having woman troubles..and it made you come all the way up here in this cold mountain, alone.."

I laughed a bleak laugh. "Not the way you mean it Ana."

"I'm so confused Edmond."

"You're not the only one."

She remained quiet for a little while not looking at me, trying to decipher what it is that was really bothering me. She was fidgeting her fingers, and looking across the barren snowy valley. While biting her lip, she looked up at me and squinted her eyes..as if she were trying to read my mind.

At that moment, I noticed that her eyes...were very large.

"You are not going to guess it Ana." I said with a sparky chuckle as I finally stood up.

"Perhaps you can give me a hint?" she asked.

And like a flash of lighting, the voice inside my head had something to say:

"Why does she **want** to know what is **going** on in your mind so **desperately**? Be **careful** my dearest **Edmond**, she might be up to something **suspicious**. Does she want some intel that she can **gossip** to **Felix** and **Josephine** about?"

Be quiet..

"She **already** knows, that you **don't** share any **feelings** for her..why can't she let this go? There must be **some** selfish **reason** as to why she keeps on..**persisting**..? A **secret** motive **perhaps**?"

"Well..?" She persisted.

"Please let it go, Ana."

But she was still persistent, I can see it in her eyes. Still speculating, still trying to understand what may be the central reason why I am perplexed, or why I have strong feelings for a stranger, and not for her. I can see confusion in her eyes, and uneasiness in her legs. Perhaps she wanted to understand why I have immense feelings for a stranger, and not for a close friend.

"I am thinking about moving away Ana." I broke open." I think I need to get out of town and start a fresh new life." I lied.

"Why?"

"Just.. because. Listen, I am young, and single. I have no wife, no children..no family, and am a man full of adventure. I like to live my life on the *edge*." I said with a smirk, trying to be funny by portraying a cheesy "bad boy demeanor."

But, this was a mistake.

She disregarded my corny endeavors.

"Where will you go Edmond? Back to Europe?"

"I don't think so.." I whispered.

But seriously, where would I go? I have no family and no friends anywhere elsewhere besides this small town. I have a few acquaintances back in Europe, but that is just about it. Other than that, I am alone.

Alone in this world full of darkness...

"You are so **dramatic** my dearest **Edmond**."

Yes I know.

Fortunately, Ana interrupted my conversation with that annoying voice inside my head.

"Are you running away?" she shouted.

Why is she always yelling?

I did not answer her question, I had no choice but to pause. No choice but to think.

Her question did spark my interest. It made me question myself for a while. Was I running away? If so...why? There was no special place or monument I wanted to see. No special person that I wanted to meet..

No matter where I was on this planet, nothing would change my perspectives. I simply would feel the same as I feel today. Feeling that no matter where I am on this planet, I simply do not belong anywhere.

Her question hit a mark in my heart. Something that I have been trying my best to run away from; and that was a certain truth. That no matter where I was, I would not be going *to anywhere*. I simply would only be running *away from somewhere*.

Was I running to somewhere new, or was I simply running away from something else? I hated not knowing the answer. I always knew that I was a fool, but when did I, Edmond James become such a coward? When did he become so confused? Edmond James never runs; and Edmond James always has an answer.

259

I sat back down in disbelief of my own self discovery. Ana's question has left paralyzed and without a verbal answer.

Yes...where would I go?

Yes..I was running away..

Ana approached my side by scooting closer to me on the rock. She then wrapped her warm slender arm around me. Upon her doing so, I flinched as if she were going to strike me; I was most paranoid of everything so far. But after perceiving that her motion was nothing more than a friendly gesture of comfort, I softened and allowed her to embrace me.

"I'm cold Edmond…"

"It **was** just a **friendly** gesture..no big **deal**."

Hopefully.

Perhaps she saw the discomfort on my face at first. But it did not matter, for at this point, her eyes were not focused on me anymore. Her eyes became fixed on the snowy mountain landscapes in front of us. As she rests her head upon my shoulder, I feel strong. I feel empowerment..

I will admit, such an experience over this mountainous valley while the snowfall is present amongst us, is quite romantic.

I must be careful-

"I don't want you to go Edmond." She whispered.

Her body language and tone of voice already gave way to such a confession. I already knew she did not want me to go. It always seems that no matter where I go, or how hard I try to be alone..she is always there. I was reading Ana like a novel ever since we met. She is a certain.. *"type."*

The "type" you can trust, but at the same time..the "type" that you can distrust. She was the woman who sought validation from men. Seeking the approval of a man, gave Ana the confidence she needed to find the approval of herself. Her own source of insecurity to security.

And I refused, to play into it.

But on a more commendable side, Ana was a loyal friend.

"If you do decide to leave, even if you feel that you are running away..I know that you'll be back." she consoled with her lost but hardly recognizable English accent. "You will return in order to face head on whatever it is that you are running away from...you're the *type*."

Her words were as real and as genuine as life and time itself. Very comforting to say the least. I felt warm hearing her words; realizing that such a person had a strong hope for me.

A hope she carried for the man she saw within, a man who she saw, was willing to take his challenges head on; a man who was not a coward.

I try to vision the strong internal character of Edmond James that she feels she knows; and reflect that image on myself, and in what my next big move would be in my life. I never once in my life doubted my ability to face challenge or difficulty. I was no quitter, nor was I a man who surrendered under pressure. That is, until I felt powerless in front of those eyes at the deli shop earlier. I was disappointed with myself, when I found myself frozen, immobilized and unable to properly approach her and order a simple soda..all confidence in myself had indeed vanished; for I was struck with fear.

What was interesting, was Ana's comment that included evidence that she has evaluated me as a certain "type."

While she evaluates me as a commendable "type," I evaluate and analyze her with a non-commendable "type."

She saw strength, while I saw weakness..And that is wrong of me.

Am I deciding to move or run away away because I feel that I am amongst the midst of an environment that I cannot endure?

261

Suppose that is the case, would Ana be wrong about my "type?" Would I be wrong if I fled, while she remained here? What is the difference between us, that I am willing to start a new life and she doesn't? Is the difference measured by internal character and strength? Does she possess more strength than I do?

Impossible..

Or, perhaps the reason is a financial reason. Perhaps I have the financial freedom to leave, while she does not? Or is it family? She has family here that she cannot leave and abandon.. while I do not share the luxury?

For some reason.. the latter gave way to a splash of sadness in my heart; for deep down, I knew that was the reason. It created within me at this moment a sensation of bitterness and anger.. and I could feel the voice inside my head begin to take over.

Without thinking, I allowed the voice inside my head to petulantly protrude a remark that I knew I would soon regret.

"I don't think you would want any man to leave you."

She quickly took her head off my shoulder and flared at me with her big, brown, yellowish eyes.

Do they change color..? Remarkable.

"What do you mean by that?" Ana cried out in defense mode.

I made a grave mistake by allowing my own insecurity consume me.

"What are you trying to say..Edmond?"

"Tell her the truth my **dearest** Edmond, tell her that you know how **desperate** she is for a man's **attention**; tell her that she is **confused**."

But we both are confused. All of us are..?

"But she is **confused** about *herself*. Not the other way **around**.

262

Tell her that you are **aware** that she **doesn't** care about you. That your **attention** towards her, gives her **validation**..just like all the other **men** in her life."

But what if I am wrong..?

"You are not **wrong**. You are never **wrong**. But **what** you are, my kind sir, is a **pawn** to the queen of the **chess** game of life. That you can see it as **clear** as day, and that to her, you are no **different** than all the **other men** that she **placed** her head on upon their **shoulders**.."

I ignore the voice of contempt and incrimination inside my head. Quickly, I vigorously shake off the battling thoughts and respond with another lie.

"What I mean Ana, is that I am not so special of a man for you to only love, and a man whom you don't want to see leave.."

I wonder if that statement will work.

She remained silent.

Try a new approach; try another lie.

"I am sorry Ana, but we both know that you are too good for me. I just..haven't found what I am looking for just yet. But I do enjoy your friendship."

"What do you mean? Do you honestly think that I would drive all the way up here, in the cold snow, and spend my time with any guy up here? I have an exam to take tomorrow and I could have used this time to study so I can pass my courses. But, no..I came out of my way in search for *you* because I was worried; because I *care about you,* and you respond to me like this.."

I detect drama among the horizon.

I should have guessed that she would feel this offended. Given the nature and status of her lingering feelings, it should have been obvious to me that she would react in this manner. But, I hadn't been prepared for her reaction in the heat of this moment, for I wasn't in my best comforts to channel my attention towards analytical thinking.

I think way too much.

"Ana, I'm sorry..I—"

"No it's ok Edmond. You keep apologizing and I forget, you have nothing to apologize for. Don't feel guilty or bad about yourself because I have romantic expectations of you; I guess.."

She looks towards the ground.

"But please, as a friend, and a damn really good friend who I never want to lose, just think a little bit more before you voice your opinion."

Upon hearing her statement I was confused yet again. But I forgive the poor soul, for she simply has no idea just how much I do think. Think about what I am going to say, and why I say what I say. She has no idea, that I filter so much activity before I voice my mind, that when speaking to others everything can become unbearable.

During our conversation she has no idea that while she spoke about our impossible romance and my absurdity of a reason to feel emotionless amongst a stranger, I was observing our surroundings. Counting the snowflakes as they fall, while observing the squirrels play near the trees to our right; I was also focusing on her, myself, what she said, why she said it, what should I say, and what I should not say. All the more, observing the fawn play with their mother about 17 meters away from us to our left. Little does Ana know, I was quite paranoid the whole time during her confessions; for if the father elk sees us so close to his mate and children, he may decide to attack us with such ferocity that she and I would not have made it to our cars alive if we were gored.

Not to mention, I noticed her scarf was crimson, which I recall reading from a source that male bucks and elks detest the color red and triggers aggression inside them. We were actually in much more danger, for we are also blissfully associating in bear and wolf territory.

This forest, conceals much danger. For this reason my heart was distracted.

It was suffocating to filter all of these disturbances while trying to calm Ana in a manner so that *she would not be offended.*

Obviously I failed.

"Are you listening to me Edmond?"

"Yes..yes I am Ana. You were saying..?"

"Nothing."

"Well...ok then.." I sighed.

"It's just—" she began.

And here we go...

"—I wish that you were more reasonable about a few things. For once, you vanish without a trace and have all of us worried—"

"'All of us?'"

"—Second, you don't tell anyone where you are and what you are doing with yourself and then you come all the way up here alone, in the snowy mountains."

I pause.

"Then you explain to me, only after I found you and force you to speak to me, that you came up here to clear your thoughts about a girl—"

Not entirely true Ana, but go ahead..

"—A gorgeous girl whom you *claim* that you don't know, and never met, but have strong feelings and attachment for and that you want to *move away..*? Now, you don't want to talk about any of it.. Do you have any idea how confusing this all sounds?" She scorned at me.

265

This is when, I had enough of her babbling and had to explain myself.

"Confusion is just the lack of understanding of a central idea Ana. Just because you do not understand the central idea, does not mean that your confusion is evidence that I am wrong about what I know or what I feel."

"Yes but—"

"Let me finish."

"I do not understand why I feel this way about a woman who I do not know. However, just because I do not know her, but I do know you, does not make you entitled to receive my romance. You are a lovely woman, full of good character and hope. As true as my statements about what makes you shine amongst the stars are true and valid, so too, are true about what it is that I am not attracted to about you."

She listened intently, as if she never seen me speak so declaratively about what I feel about her. In fact, she never did actually hear my side of what I feel towards her.

"There are many other things on my mind that I cannot speak of to you. Not because I don't want to, believe me, I do. But you simply cannot understand, and for that reason, I cannot speak of what is on my mind; also for that same reason I also don't want to."

"Edmond I'm confu—"

"Now, what I am saying does not mean that I do not value you as a human being, person or friend. But understand, that you came up here on this cold, snowy mountain by your own choice, if I wanted you here I would have called you. You came during one of my darkest hours, and I was not prepared to speak about my life story with anyone, not even you. By you forcing me into a conversation, you were forcing me into a corner.."

My mouth twisted and molded with chagrin. I did not like hurting Ana by confusing her about our relationship. But the truth of the matter is, is that we had no relationship, other than our friendship. I do care about Ana, but not in a romantic sense. How could I? For I know her feelings for me in a romantic sense were not completely genuine. Her "feelings" she has for me, were not deep, hardly pure..so how could I ever return something that is not romantically authentic?

She was pressuring me into delivering my feelings about what was on my mind as if she deserved to learn about them. On the basis of friendship, I do not feel that friendship is a concession to the revealing of all secrets.

Perhaps this is selfish of me.

"Ok Edmond, I get it..you're right." she mumbled in disappointment. "It was not fair for me to push you in the direction of a conversation that you did not want to go."

Yes, that is right.

"Maybe...maybe I should go then."

"No, you do not have to leave-"

"Let her leave my dearest **Edmond**. She has made you upset, and **destroyed** the peace that you **came** out here for..she **would** be doing you a **kindness** if she left—"

But she was trying to be nice..trying to be a good friend..

"No my **kind** sir, she was trying to see if she was **important** enough for you to reveal secrets. She was **measuring** her value, based upon if she could **break** your silence. Your **presence**, was the **attention** that she so craved..Not **because** she wants and values your time..but only because she feels some **stimulus** when she is around you—a level of self **confirmation**."

The voice inside my head was right. Ana Christine was a certain type. The type that would go to an extreme measure to seek a man's approval. Her past actions and experience that I became witness to fueled this testimony. But still, Ana was a good person, and I did not want to hurt her..

She stood up.

"Edmond..?"

"Yes, I think you should go. It's getting dark, and the temperature will drop tremendously." I voiced my honest concern for her well being.

"Are you going home too..?" she said.

I look up.

"The skies are clear this night, I think if I stay a bit longer, I will have a chance to see their wonder."

"So is that a no..? Are you staying out here..or?"

I sighed.

"Yes Ana. That means that I am staying out—here." I pointed to the rock where we sat and where we bonded over the past year. We would sit on this rock and star gaze during the warm summer nights. The stars in this area are absolutely magical.

"Well, I guess I will be on my way. I am glad that you are well and ok Edmond, that is all I wanted to know.."

I gave her a corny thumbs up.

She walked over towards me in order to give me a hug goodbye.

She warmly embraced me as if she tripped over a log allowing me to catch her.

She held onto me like she and I would never see each other again.

She held on tight..

"Will I see you around?" She asked.

"Of course." I lied, my eyes piercing through her innocent marbled stone pupils.

Five seconds.

"Ok, well text me when you get home safely Edmond."

"I will."

Ten seconds.

"You promise?"

"I promise." I lied.

Twenty seconds.

She sighed deeply, and finally let go of me.

"Well, if you decide to move away before we see each other..goodbye Edmond."

We stopped embracing each other, and upon doing so, she hesitantly turned around to walk away. It was at that moment, that something inside me told me to kiss her; *and I did.* I kissed her on the cheek, pulling back swiftly as she slowly twisted her face towards mine; her lips already puckered in an attempt to kiss and embrace the sensation of mine. A sensation and pleasure, that she unknowingly could not handle.

Embarrassed, she smiled and turned around to walk away.

"Goodbye Ana."

She didn't say a word.

"Thank you for coming, I needed to hear your words."

Once again, she didn't say a word, nor did she even look back at me. She vanished swiftly through the snowy glaze before us; like a ghost phantomizing through the crisp cold air. Nightfall was approaching this snowy valley, and the snowflakes decided to morph into soft rain.

How dramatic.

My rejection bothered her, I could feel that it did. But Ana was a persistent woman, and I knew that one day when we cross paths again, she might try to win me over. Perhaps, one day she might..that is, if I can clear my thoughts of anxiousness over the other girl.

All things aside, I am glad that Ana left. She would return home safe and sound, and deliver the message to Felix and Josephine that I was ok, saving me from experiencing the trouble. I sat back on the rock from which Ana and I resided and placed my chin upon my knees. The stars were beginning to appear over the horizon, and soon, my eyes would become graced with the beauty of the expansion of the universe. Such peace..such tranquility. For the first time today, I felt like I could finally breathe.

Although truthfully, I was anxious to be on my way home; it has been a long day. However, I felt that I was already at home. Alone on this mountain, with the stars above, I felt warm and comfortable, as if lying in my bed; while the stars of heaven were a blanket that soothed my burning soul.

I wonder what it must feel like to pray?

Pray to a God who I feel may not even consider my feelings..

In any sense, I was alone again, and the peace that I was searching for was finally within my grasp.

thank you for reading
please follow my
instagram profile
im order to stay updated
for this book's official release!

follow
hewett.vision

questions and answers
you asked,
and
i answered

samantha mcdaniel
q: "who or what inspired you to start writing poetry? i know that may seem like a basic question, but i always find it fascinating to know the person's story on how they began doing something they have a passion for."

a: it is not a basic question at all. thank you. poetry allows me to express my emotions in a way that feels comfortable. there was a time, where my extreme feelings remained unvoiced; there existed no one i could talk to about it, and i was left alone, to deal with them in my own way. so, i wrote my thoughts and feelings down on paper which became the skeleton for many of my projects.

natale gomez
q: "what inspired you to write?"

a: very similar answer to the question raised above. however to this question, i will say that i was inspired to write, because i found that writing is an art; and art i feel, connects humanity. i wanted to share in this connection with those who have a voice, but aren't too sure on how to speak in a way, i am inspired because i want to help.

anthony manuel
q: "what hardship did you experience in life that ultimately lead to writing and becoming and author?"

a: nice question, there was a time in my young life when i found myself alone. famous author stephen king once said that authors are not born, they are created, molded by their environment; and i couldn't agree more. i found that i existed in solitude, namely because i had a circle of friends, who i felt just did not understand my vision. i could not express myself because they could never walk in my shoes. as a result, i remained speechless, until i could not hold it in any longer..and then, i began to write my thoughts down. there are good days, and bad days, but, my desire to become a published author was stronger. good question

rosie nunez
q: "why is such a handsome, and romantic guy like yourself single?"

a: ooh i like this question! well i suppose that i am single because i have not prepared myself to give my all to one woman. by "give my all," i mean that i am not ready to sacrifice for one person. i think a man must be ready to give himself to a particular woman. i have not found that woman just yet who is worthy. also, i have not had anyone be authentic or genuine in the past, nor found someone whose mind i am currently attracted to just yet.

jacob maisel
q: "where did your love for poetry and writing begin? any particular moment, layout in life?"

a: yes. when i was in the second grade, i wrote a poem about a rhino that wasn't allowed to drink at the watering hole in the safari.

the poem was actually a story, about how the rhino didn't want to hurt anyone, but, simply wanted some water to drink. the other animals were afraid of him, and would not let him drink because of his large horn. i received great feedback from almost every teacher in my school. i believe that was the start of it all.

tamata kasnioska
q: "any of the poems based on your life? and are you writing for a lost love of yours?"

a: the poems and stories i write spring from unspoken expressions towards a particular individual. there exists one woman, who i was so much in love with, that i lost focus on who and what i am. i was haunted by her absence; my obsession caused her to erupt inside of my dreams nearly almost night, and it was then that she became "the angel in my nightmares" it was my desire to speak to her once again, that fueled my passion for writing. much of my writings really are expressions i wanted to convey to her. and her absence created the unspoken voice.
also, too, my poems have been aided by learning from a relationship i was in, in which we were right for each other, but the timing was bad. i was in a bad place in my mind, and i caused many issues that resulted in our breakups.

priya singh
q: "why is it called, "romantic propaganda?"

a: great question! no one has ever asked that question before. the book is called, "romantic propaganda" because in my "letters to men," "letters to women," and "letters to no one," i address social issues in what i feel prevents people from embracing true love. in these letters, both men, and women are able to possess a more depthful vision of what it means to love the other, and to love themselves. i expose the propaganda that exists in the world today: that love is determined by superficial quality and expectations, and that we are not worthy of genuine love and satisfaction

tiffani abate
q: "what fueled your passion to continue writing?"

a: through all the ups and downs, i at times felt like giving up on myself. having no motivation to start my day. having no motivation to believe in myself. writing has allowed me to climb myself out of the hole of my self pity because i understood that my words were something that could help people. once i understood that, i began to muster the courage and continue writing; for i knew that there was someone, somewhere out there that was searching for the words that i had to say.

makenzie evangelisto
a: "you walk into a coffee shop and see the love of your life. you've never met before, and instantly you know he/she is the one. what is the very first sentence you formulate in your head and commit to from your lips?

a: interesting question. let's see..if, i were to be at a coffee shop, good chances are, that i'll be writing, or editing my books or my photos. if, she were to suddenly walk in, (and somehow i know she is the one) i would look up at her and smile. if the flare in her eyes spoke to me, and i conform to the social custom in my culture to "approach" the woman first, i would tactfully ask her for her opinion about a certain random project piece that i am working on. however, knowing that she already adores me, she will most likely find interest in it anyway. from there, i would talk to her, and get to know her name. internally, i would say to her, "i have been searching for eyes like yours." but, will say myself, "at last, bone of my bones, and flesh of my flesh." which is a quote from the first man adam; the first poem/prose found in the bible.

duaa waseem
q: "i really wanted to ask this question: in today's world do you think real love does exist, or the confluent love took over the real love relationships. even if true love does exist, what is the ratio of true love to confluent love? and, do you think women are treated as a proper human being, without any gender discrimination. if there is no gender discrimination or if it is minimized compared to old world, why are women expected to play the emotional role in a family?"

a: to answer your question i will first declare that i am no feminist, nor am i an activist of any sort. i do not get involved with topics that i feel causes division between people. in response to whether or nor not true love exists, in itself or over confluent love, i will say "yes," true love does exist. my thoughts? i believe, that "true love" is relative, and that western culture has had an ethnocentric approach and impact on what the definition of what "true love is." what an american from california defines as "true love," will differ from what someone from central africa defines as "true love." each definition or idea of what "true love is," will therefore be a reflection of cultural belief, expectation and necessity in a particular region. i take love, just the same as i take beauty: "it is in the eye of the beholder[s]" however, there is a common ground that i feel exist in all cultures as an ingredient for true love's existence; and that is respect, dignity and honor. without these three things, love cannot exist.

in response to your second question, about whether i think women are treated as a proper human being, without any gender discrimination, i will say "yes, and no." when you say, "treated as a proper human being," i will say "definitely yes." in many circumstances throughout time, women have been praised for their existence. women have served as queens, princesses, doctors, war heroes, humanitarians, soldiers; as mothers and as grandmothers even. in past times, in the western world, it was custom to not yell, scream, threat or even strike a woman. not because it is felt that she is weaker, but because women were praised, honored and well respected. for this reason, women and children were evacuated first when the titanic sunk. yet, the very opposite is also true: women have not been treated as proper human beings. this is a fact and is what it is. women definitely have been subjected to discrimination, oppression and victim hood. i believe however, that no matter what your gender is, what your race or background is, if you put your mind to it, you will overcome any obstacle the world throws at you. but, i feel women do have a much more difficult struggle than men.

to answer your final question, i would argue with the word: "expected." due to the differences in culture as previously mentioned, what is "expected," will differ from region to region.

yes, i feel, that women are "expected" to provide emotional security within the family because i feel that women are natural nurturers. i also feel that providing emotional security does not register weakness in any way, as some like to declare that it is. a man can provide emotional security as well, and in my opinion he should strive to do so. it just so happens, that women have evidently proved that they are able to be more in tune with their emotions than men are. i feel, that women are expected to confirm to more emotional roles because women are "expected" to behave more motherly than a man is. in my experience, i have seen women in my circle, actually *want* to nurture men. but, it cannot be said for all.

in my own experience, i have known women to be more emotionally driven than men are. i do believe that roles do exist. just like the man is as well expected to pay for dinners, dates, and provide protection like physical and financial security. this too is considered a role. i for one do not agree with this standard any more than i agree to the standards that a wife should stay at home. i believe roles exist, but i do not feel that "roles" are absolute. the husband can cook, clean, and conform to more house duties than the wife. relationships are a *team effort.*

dr ogundeyi emmanuel lucas
q: "how long did it take you to finish this project, and was there a time that you felt that you've done enough? "the book is done," feeling and how did you feel at that point?

a: it took me three years to finish this book. many times, i felt that the book was finished, and that i was "done." however, many circumstances in my life have arisen, that became the fuel for more inspiration that created more pages within this book. i have many other projects in the work at this moment. a romance novel is in the work as well. i have good days and bad days, combined with writer's block puts me behind schedule too. time is a value; and you cannot rush art.

murli kanne
q: "what makes you unique?"

a: i am not unique. i am as average and normal as you, or anyone
else. i feel what separates us, is not uniqueness, but is "difference."
what makes me different from others? i made a choice to never
surrender to failure. i made a choice, to love myself, and share my
talents with the world. through this, i am able to grow, and apply
myself because my choice to share myself with others has plugged
me into a realm that forces me to engage; and thus, i am different
than i was yesterday, the day before etc. this is how i grow. this is
what makes me different.

carmen guzman
a: "have you ever been lied to or cheated on? if so how did you
overcome it, how did you heal your heart? this happens to women;
we hear it often. we don't hear it from men that often. men do get
hurt, and they get taken advantage of.

a: yes i have. i have been cheated on emotionally and physically. i
had one person cheat on me with one of my closest friends physically.
i felt cheated on, when the one and only woman i loved, founded an
intimate friendship with one of my closest male friends, and left me
in the dust. in both circumstances, i felt second place. i overcame
depression and feelings of inadequacy by making the choice to define
myself, and not let the outcome of a failed relationship define me. i
made the choice that i was going to love myself. i was not going to
allow the reciprocation of my love effort, play a factor on how
important i am.

you are right. men are cheated on all the time; they just don't speak
about it. i also feel that such a thing doesn't reach mass exposure; so
we think it doesn't exist. when it comes to healing, sometimes,
people fall into the trap of believing that they will never find
someone who will make them feel as special or unique ever again.
that is a lie. you will find someone who will make you feel important
again. you will find someone who will treat you better

olanreqaju oranyeli
q: "why is it that most of your work is themed around the
emancipation of women and relationships?"

a: honestly, it is not my intent to portray such an image. i never
thought that i was writing to emancipate women, or set them free
from any social bondage as such something a feminist would so or
do. i just speak from my heart words that i would say to my sister or
daughter. i do understand that we are living in gender sensitive times,
and that both men and women are victims to gender roles. in my
"letters to men," i feel that i am emancipating men, from the bondage
of their gender roles, expectations, and imperfections; now that i have
room to think about it.

mariza rodriguez
q: "is it only personal experience you write about or do you tie
friends and family experience after you help them through whatever
it is? or while writing do you ever get touched or get emotional?
because some of your stuff really touches me

a: well, to answer your question it is half and half. some of my poetry
comes from personal experience and the other half is all based upon
what i feel inside my heart; and just wanted to voice. i don't get too
emotional when i write. i don't cry or get too emotionally involved. i
just write what i feel..and i am glad that it touches you.

angel garcia
q: "can you describe the perfect poem?"

a: i feel, that the perfect poem conveys the most honest of all feelings.
it is an unrestrained pattern of voice, that is used to move the hearts
and minds of its readers.

kyler jones
q: how do you feel about instagram poetry? and where do you feel
you fit in with other instagram poets?

a: i honestly, am not a fan of instagram poetry, although ironically i am considered an instagram poet. i am not too bright about it, because i feel a good majority of instagram poets change the direction of what i consider *real* poetry. i've seen some poets say something like: "her eyes were like the sun," or "she found herself amongst the stars.." i like to ask myself, "what does that even mean?" but, because a certain instagram poet has a high follower count and like ratio, their poetry *becomes good* rather than actually being good. anyone can splash a few pretty words on a piece of paper and call it, "poetry." many instagram poets have taken advantage of people's lack of understanding and difference from what "quotes," and what "poetry" is.

use these few blank pages to scribble out your thoughts!

Made in the USA
Las Vegas, NV
02 December 2020

11906733R00164